W9-AZK-384

Second Edition. | January 20, 2023.

Living Waters for Christ Inc.
3675 Park Avenue, Suite 101
Ellicott City, MD 21043
ablazefamily.org | setusablaze.tv

A special thanks to additional contributors:
Fr. Erik Arnold
Dr. Pat Fosarelli
Craig Gould
Javier Plumey
Merry Salamida
Maureen Schafer
Joe Schuberth
Abigail Pfau Tringali

Book design by Abigail Pfau Tringali

All Scripture passages referenced in this publication originate from the New International Version of the Bible.

Table of Contents

"It is Jesus that **you seek** when you dream of **happiness.** **He** is waiting for **you** when nothing else you find **satisfies you...** it is **He** who provoked you with that **thirst for fullness"**

Pope St. John Paul II

Part 1

This Series and How to Use It

I. Introduction

If you know anything about newborn babies, you know that they want to eat. And eat. And *eat*. New parents literally spend hours and hours each day of those first weeks just feeding the baby; it's a full-time job!

This is how you started your life too, of course. God designed our bodies and created each of us with a complex system of built-in reflexes and hunger cues to help us survive, thrive, and eventually discover the joy and importance of eating.

But sometimes something happens, and our bodies don't work the way they are supposed to.

A few years ago we welcomed baby #4, Seamus Joseph, to our family. Like all parents of newborns, we spent hours upon hours feeding our hungry little bundle of joy.

Until suddenly one day, when he was about six weeks old, he just...stopped. He stopped opening his mouth. He stopped crying when he was hungry. He stopped eating entirely. We know that babies sometimes go through spurts when they don't want to eat, but this was different. Something wasn't right.

We worked so hard to keep him nourished, but he wasn't thriving; he was just surviving. And the same was true for our whole family. This was so taxing. We solicited the help of anyone and everyone we could think of, but at a year old, Seamus wasn't showing any signs of being willing to eat, and we couldn't live like this anymore.

We needed more help.

So we were sent off to feeding therapy. We had never even heard of that, but at our first appointment we discovered a world of parents, kids, doctors, psychologists, speech pathologists and more, all working together to help people connect their hunger with the food that satisfies.

Through it all, the Lord was revealing something to us. Seamus needed help overcoming a disconnect so that his hunger would be reoriented and do what it should: lead him to desire to eat. Just so, all of us need help overcoming our spiritual disconnect so that we can recognize our hunger and allow it to be reoriented and do what it is supposed to do: lead us to desire to encounter the only thing that will ever satisfy it.

Jeremiah 29:11

"For I know the plans I have for you," declares the Lord, "plans to prosper you and not to harm you, plans to give you hope and a future."

God created us on purpose, with a purpose, because He loves us and wants us to live life to the full: an eternal, personal relationship with Him. A relationship that gives us life, that nourishes us so that we grow and thrive.

He wants this relationship with each of us, and He wants us to desire it too. So, He created us with a built-in hunger for Himself.

But something happened.

Through Adam and Eve, sin entered our world, and each of us has inherited it. Sin causes a disconnect; our hunger for God is still there, but it's disoriented. Because of sin, we become restless and seek satisfaction in anything and everything other than God, to no avail. We desperately need help if we are going to not just survive but thrive spiritually.

God loves us so much that He made a plan. He sent His only begotten Son, Jesus, to become one of us, to suffer, die, and rise again in order to save us. Jesus has ransomed and rescued us from sin and death and has restored our capacity for Himself and for the abundant, full life that He offers.

Sin still disorients us, but Jesus gives us His Holy Spirit to guide and help us: to re-orient our hunger so that we can ultimately experience the satisfaction of encountering the Lord and responding to Him in a way that satisfies.

We call this process *Spiritual Feeding Therapy*.

We can cooperate with the Holy Spirit in offering **Spiritual Feeding Therapy** by tending and guiding souls in our own families and parish families.

This is the One Best Thing: to encounter the Lord, experience the satisfaction and joy that only He can give, and respond to Him in a way that leads to a life of ever-more-wonderful encounters and responses, all the way to eternity. In this, we become our truest, most alive, most joyful selves. And it is **Spiritual Feeding Therapy** that allows this to happen.

We are delighted to join you as the Holy Spirit guides and involves each of us in this process.

Kristen and Greg Fisher

Register Your book

1. Open the camera app on your phone and hold it over the QR code to scan. Or visit *https://ablz.org/tobt-videos*.
2. Once redirected to the One Best Thing Hub, create an account if prompted.
3. Select the "Video Series" tab and click the teal "Get Started" button.
4. When you're ready, click the "Next" button at the bottom of the page to start watching the first video chapter.
5. Continue reading and enjoy access to the videos in the following chapters, the hubs, and more resources!

Scan here

II. How to Use This Series

In this series, we'll walk with you as you explore the one **best** thing that any of us could possibly have, the one thing that leads to living life to the full. And we'll share a practical, personal process you can use to offer it over and over to your kids.

Each step is its own chapter and will start with a video (available via QR code and the link listed on each section page), and then it will offer a summary followed by reflection questions and practical guidance on how to apply that step. We recommend that you use this guidance to learn more about yourself first (because you also have this need for the **One Best Thing**, even if you've never recognized it before), and then apply it to your kids and your family. The process includes:

- The One Best Thing: Living Our Best Lives (p. 9-11)
- Recognizing Our Deepest Hunger (p. 12-14)
- Setting a Goal (p. 15-17)
- Building Trust, Modeling, and a "Cloud of Witnesses" (p. 18-21)
- Preference Patterns and a Balanced Diet (p. 22-35)
- Becoming Food for the World (p. 36-41)
- Personalizing This Process (p. 42-47)

Just as most things in life are more enjoyable and more fruitful when done with others, we encourage you to go through this series with others: other parents, other grandparents, teachers, ministers, coaches, and other people who love kids and want what's best for them, just like you.

Because this is a handbook, a reference and guide rather than a novel, you'll find that roughly ⅔ of it is made up of three appendices, full of practical guidance to help you to apply what you've learned in a way that is personal and relevant to the actual people in your family. Be sure to check those out—more than a dozen moms and dads, ministers and therapists, educators and coaches contributed to those sections and we think you'll find them to be very helpful.

We're so happy to share with you what we've learned along the way, and we're honored to stand alongside you as we offer our kids the very best.

Part 2

Offering the One Best Thing

Chapter I. The One Best Thing: Living Our Best Lives

https://ablz.org/tobt-videos

St. Augustine

"God is always trying to give good things to us, but our hands are too full to receive them."

After watching the video linked above, ask the Holy Spirit to help you use the content below to reflect and apply it to your own life.

Key takeaways

1. As parents, we all want our kids to have a good life. While there are many good experiences, opportunities, and gifts that we can give them, there is only *One Best Thing*. No matter the circumstances, we can all offer this to them.

2. St. Augustine lived a life filled with all that the world could offer and accomplished all he could on his own, but he was still unsatisfied, wandering in search of what would truly satisfy. When he finally encountered the Lord personally in the Scriptures, he found what he was looking for. He traded the life that he had, for abundant life (which only the Lord can give).

3. Augustine's story is our story; we were made by God, for God, and only He can truly satisfy our wandering hearts and help us become who we're meant to be. This is *The One Best Thing*: an encounter with the Lord that satisfies and brings joy. It is in living a life full of these encounters, and responding to them, which allows us to experience "life to the full" as Jesus promised.[1]

Reflection

- Like Augustine, most of us probably think to ourselves, "I'll finally be happy when _____." What is that thing that you've chased (or are currently chasing) that you thought would satisfy? Have you (like Augustine) ever obtained it, only to find that it didn't satisfy?

- Have you ever experienced God's love in a way that was obvious to you? What was that satisfaction like?

"**You** have **made us** for **yourself** **O, LORD,** and our **hearts** **are restless** until they **rest** **in YOU.**"

St. Augustine

Notes, Thoughts, and Reflections

Chapter II. Our Deepest Hunger: Seamus' Story

C.S. Lewis, *Mere Christianity*

Watch Now!

https://ablz.org/tobt-videos

"If I find in myself a desire which no experience in this world can satisfy, the most probable explanation is that I was made for another world...Probably earthly pleasures were never meant to satisfy it, but only to arouse it, to suggest the real thing. If that is so, I must take care, on the one hand, never to despise these earthly blessings, and on the other, never to mistake them for the something else of which they are only a kind of copy, or echo, or mirage." [2]

After watching the video linked above, ask the Holy Spirit to help you use the content below to reflect and apply it to your own life.

Key takeaways

1. The Lord gave us built-in reminders to "be fed"— our physical hunger leads us to eat food, and spiritual hunger motivates us to seek and be satisfied by Him. Sin distorts and distracts us from our built-in hunger, so like Augustine, we wander in search of something else that satisfies, to no avail.

2. Jesus came to suffer, die, and rise again to free us from sin, and He now invites us to encounter and respond to Him, that we might have life to the full, on Earth and ultimately in Eternity. The life that Jesus offers begins at Baptism when God comes to actually dwell in us. [3]

3. Seamus' feeding journey is a parable of sorts: he needed help recognizing that food was the answer to his hunger. Similarly, we all need help recognizing that God alone is the answer to our spiritual hunger and restlessness. Just as food is essential for our bodies to survive and thrive, encountering and being fed by the Lord is *essential* for our spiritual lives.

4. As it was for St. Augustine, it is through personal, authentic encounter with the Lord that we experience satisfaction that changes everything, a taste of life to the full that Jesus promised. This encounter enables us to become who we were created to be, and motivates us to keep coming back to the Lord as the source of life.

"God loves each of us as if there were only one of us."

Reflection

The Lord offers each of us what nobody and nothing else can.

Jesus suffered, died, and rose again in order to rescue us from our restless wandering caused by sin, so that we could ultimately be in a relationship with Him here on Earth and forever in Heaven. He did this, not just for all of us in general, but for each of us, personally.

- What does it mean for you, that God loves your children even more than you do?

- St. Paul tells us that Scripture is "living and effective"; God is actively speaking to us through it today. Which of the Scripture passages below resonates most with you and your deepest hunger?

John 6:35

"I am the bread of life; whoever comes to me will never go hungry, and whoever believes in me will never be thirsty."

Psalm 63:1-3

"You, God, are my God, earnestly I seek you; I thirst for you, my whole being longs for you, in a dry and parched land where there is no water. I have seen you in the sanctuary and beheld your power and your glory. Because your love is better than life, my lips will glorify you."

Mark 8:36

"What does it profit a man to gain the whole world, yet forfeit his soul?"

Notes, Thoughts, and Reflections

Chapter III. Setting a Goal

Watch Now!

https://ablz.org/tobt-videos

Antoine de Saint-Exupery

"A goal without a plan is just a wish."

After watching the video linked above, ask the Holy Spirit to help you use the content below to reflect and apply it to your own life.

Key takeaways

1. Creating a goal helps us articulate what matters most, what we most deeply desire for ourselves and our children. It helps us live intentionally and measure our daily choices against that which we desire most.

2. Our goal can't simply be for our children to adopt certain behaviors (i.e. "We want Seamus to eat food"); we actually want them to desire good for themselves (i.e. "We want Seamus to *want* to eat food"). We must help them experience the satisfaction that a real encounter with the Lord offers, so that they join us in desiring *the One Best Thing* for themselves.[4]

3. In all of the goal-setting that we do for our kids, we find peace and strength in remembering that God's greatest desire is for us to know Him personally, and to respond to and cooperate with His love. He came so that we might have life to the full; it was His idea long before it was ours. He pursues each of us long before we seek Him. Our goals and plans of helping others encounter and respond to Him are in cooperation with His great plan of salvation.[5]

Reflection

We need to start by establishing an end goal and by being honest about where we are now. Then, we can create a plan to get from where we are right now, to where we want to be.

"Our aim has to be the infinite and not the finite. The infinite has always been our homeland."

Reflection continued

- What is your ultimate, eternal goal for your family?

- Where are you starting?
  - What in your life is already consistent with this goal?
  - What in your life is inconsistent with this goal?
  - What in your life is currently neutral, but could potentially become helpful or unhelpful, if it were prioritized differently?

The next 3 chapters will identify aspects of a spiritual feeding therapy plan to work toward your goal, no matter where you are starting from.

Matthew 6:19-21

"Do not store up for yourselves treasures on earth, where moths and vermin destroy, and where thieves break in and steal. But store up for yourselves treasures in heaven, where moths and vermin do not destroy, and where thieves do not break in and steal. For where your treasure is, there your heart will be also."

Notes, Thoughts, and Reflections

Chapter IV. Building Trust, Modeling, and a Cloud of Witnesses

Colossians 3:12-14

Watch Now!

https://ablz.org/tobt-videos

"Therefore, as God's chosen people, holy and dearly loved, clothe yourselves with compassion, kindness, humility, gentleness and patience. Bear with each other and forgive one another if any of you has a grievance against someone. Forgive as the Lord forgave you. And over all these virtues put on love, which binds them all together in perfect unity."

After watching the video linked above, ask the Holy Spirit to help you use the content below to reflect and apply it to your own life.

Key takeaways

1. **Building trust** helps us to have influence, as was the case with Bethany and Seamus. Trust is rooted in relationship: spending time together, caring about what the other cares about, playing together, and sharing experiences.[6]

2. Trust allows us to **model** the desired behavior, which helps our children see that the Lord makes an actual difference when we (like Augustine) go beyond simply learning about Him, to encountering Him personally.

3. We need to partner our modeling with talking about our faith. It's not one or the other; it's **both** modeling **and** talking that bears the most fruit.[7]

4. Parents are the most influential relationship in their childrens' lives, but they aren't the only influence.[8] All of us benefit from having a **cloud of witnesses**—other people who journey with us and bear witness to the life-changing difference that the **One Best Thing** makes. In particular, children need other adults, in addition to their parents, with whom they can talk openly about faith.[9]

Reflection (It's okay if you don't yet have answers to all of these.)

BUILDING TRUST

- When it comes to building trust, one of the ***best*** ways is to have fun and spend quality time with our children through building what social scientists call "warm family relationships."*(10)* How is that already happening with your children now?

- ***Building trust*** requires observing and listening. How do you let your children know that you are listening and paying attention?

Research has repeatedly shown that eating dinner together as a family benefits every member of the family physically, emotionally, spiritually, mentally.*(11)* It's one of the best ways to build trust and deepen family bonds. We recommend making family dinners part of your family culture, if they aren't already.

MODELING

Research shows that our kids benefit not just when we teach them about faith, but also when we talk about our own personal experience of faith, all while living in a way that demonstrates it too.

- How do you ***currently model*** that ***the One Best Thing*** is actually the one, best thing in your life? How do you already talk about your faith with your kids?

- How can you help your children know that you are a "work in progress" too?

Ephesians 4:1-2

"I urge you to live a life worthy of the calling you have received. Be completely humble and gentle; be patient, bearing with one another in love."

19

CLOUD OF WITNESSES

In the letter to the Hebrews, St. Paul talks about a *cloud of witnesses*, other people who walk with us in faith. This includes people on Earth and saints in Heaven, young and old, all of whom can accompany, support, and join us in modeling to help our children encounter and respond to the Lord. More than just friends or supporters of our families and our kids, these individuals offer us friendship and support that is rooted in Christ.

- Who do you have (adults and kids) in your life *right now* who are part of your *cloud of witnesses*?

- How can you make spending time with these individuals a priority, so that they can deepen their relationship with and join you in being spiritual models and accompaniment for others?

Never underestimate the power of prayer. Pray that the Lord will help you to find holy friends to be part of your *cloud of witnesses*! He wants this even more than we do.

St. Teresa
of Ávila

"What a great favor God does to those He places in the company of good people!"

Notes, Thoughts, and Reflections

Chapter V. Preference Patterns and a Balanced Diet

Watch Now!

https://ablz.org/tobt-videos

Psalm 63:1

"You, God, are my God, earnestly I seek you; I thirst for you, my whole being longs for you."

After watching the video linked above, ask the Holy Spirit to help you use the content below to reflect and apply it to your own life.

Key takeaways

1. Observing and listening to our kids helps us recognize patterns in their preferences, which then helps us better understand how to guide them to encounter the Lord in a way that is particularly satisfying for them.

2. There are universal ways in which the Lord feeds all of us, like the Sacraments of the Church. But there are also ways that are more personal.

3. Our built-in spiritual hunger manifests in a particular "flavor preference" or "craving." This preferred flavor can help us experience the Lord in a truly satisfying way and motivate us to keep encountering Him.[11] The three main flavors that we might crave are *Beauty, Truth, and Goodness,* and they all find their fullness in the Lord Himself.

4. We can help our kids become aware of their hunger for God by helping them to personally experience the difference that encountering Him makes. We can gently redirect their hunger toward Him, offer lots of opportunities to encounter Him (like offering Seamus a plate of food at every meal), and invite them to "taste and see," discovering how satisfying His love is for themselves (Psalm 34:8).

5. Like St. Monica did for Augustine, the greatest gift we can give to our kids is to pray with and for them, that they will be open to all the Lord wants to give them. In this way, we remember that God alone—who loves them even more than we do—is powerful enough to change hearts and minds.[12]

"Lord Jesus, let me know myself and know you."

Reflection

Our next section will guide you to recognize some potential preference patterns that are related to your each of your children's attributes and inclinations. But you might also see some patterns already, in yourself and in them. Patterns help us to know something more about ourselves, to see how the Lord created us, and how He might be trying to get our attention.
Holy Spirit, help us to know ourselves and our children.

- What consistently makes you feel motivated or inspired?
  - How might this be part of the way God made you, on purpose, with a purpose?
  - How might this be part of the way God is trying to get your attention through your own particular hunger?

- What consistently makes each of your kids feel motivated or inspired?
  - How might this be part of the way God made them, on purpose with a purpose?
  - How might this be part of the way God is trying to get their attention through their own particular hunger?
  - How is God inviting you to gently guide each of them in this way?

Proverbs 22:6

"Start children off on the way they should go, and even when they are old they will not turn from it."

Notes, Thoughts, and Reflections

V(A). Using Preference Patterns to Find the Right First Food

Ralph Waldo Emerson

"Truth, and goodness, and beauty, are but different faces of the same all."

Just as the Lord created our bodies with built-in hunger to signal us when it's time to eat, He created our souls with a built-in hunger system too. This hunger makes us feel restless and leads us to search for something that satisfies (in different ways for each of us).

Our spiritual hunger is like a particular flavor preference; we are hungry in general, but something specific is especially appealing to each of us. This flavor is likely to be the most satisfying, and we are often most naturally drawn to it, at least initially.

Just as we need to be physically nourished so that we can grow and thrive, we need to be spiritually nourished to grow and thrive too, so that we can experience life to the full.

3 basic flavors

1. When it comes to being satisfied by the Lord, the different flavors we crave are actually aspects of Who God is, and they can be boiled down to the 3 classic transcendentals: ***Beauty, Truth, and Goodness***. God is Beauty itself, Truth itself, and Goodness itself, in their fullness. [13] Everything that is beautiful, true, or good points to Him and can lead us to Him, if we let it. [14]

2. When we discover the way our particular preference craving manifests, we can know how the Lord might be trying to get our attention; remember, He desires to encounter us personally long before we even think of it! This flavor preference will also likely give insight into how the Lord wants to be at work in and through us to share His love with others. [15]

3. Just as delicious food both satisfies and stirs up our appetite, an encounter with the Lord that is satisfying will help us to want to encounter Him again and again and respond to His love, because we've seen and felt the difference that He makes in our lives.

A balanced, steady diet

When young children are learning to eat, finding a favorite food can often help open the door to eating in general. Similarly, encountering God in and through the flavor we most prefer can and should help open wide the doors of our hearts to Him more fully. The goal, of course, is to ultimately consume a "balanced diet" so that we can encounter and be nourished by the Lord in His fullness.

Just as it would not be healthy to eat our favorite foods and flavors exclusively, we each need to be nourished fully in spiritual life as well. We need to see our preferred way of encountering the Lord for what it is: a gateway to ultimately welcoming every way in which He comes. Since ***God is Beauty, Truth, and Goodness itself,*** those flavors can never truly be separated from each other, just experienced in different concentrations.

Remember: real Beauty, Truth, and Goodness are distinct, but they are never separate from or in conflict with one another. While we are likely inclined and attracted to one more than another, the one we prefer should lead us to the others, as they are all part of the same whole.

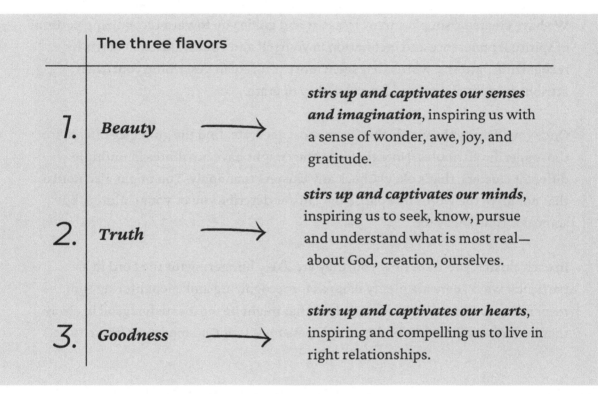

The three flavors

1. **Beauty** ⟶ ***stirs up and captivates our senses and imagination**, inspiring us with a sense of wonder, awe, joy, and gratitude.*

2. **Truth** ⟶ ***stirs up and captivates our minds**, inspiring us to seek, know, pursue and understand what is most real— about God, creation, ourselves.*

3. **Goodness** ⟶ ***stirs up and captivates our hearts**, inspiring and compelling us to live in right relationships.*

Dr. Peter Kreeft

"All that is clear (to me, anyway) is that beauty, like truth and goodness, is divinely designed to be food for our souls; that is why He designed in us an innate and universal hunger for it." [16]

V(B). The One Best Thing Instrument: Overview

There are many tests and surveys available to assist people in understanding themselves, their interests, and their personalities. Each assessment or tool helps the user gain insight into the way he or she was made and the way in which he or she operates.

We have created a simple survey to assist and guide you toward recognizing patterns of spiritual preference and inclination in yourself and your children. It starts by recognizing patterns: words that seem most accurate in describing your/their attributes, inclinations, and how you/they operate.

Once you identify the words that seem most accurate, find the guidance offered for those specific attributes. Note that you/they might have attributes in multiple different clusters; that's okay! Check any clusters that apply. You might also notice that not *all* of the words in a particular cluster describe you or your children, but some do. That's okay too.

In each cluster, you'll see how you/they are likely hungering for the Lord in a particular way. There are plenty of ideas for recognizing and encountering Him, responding to Him, and sharing His love that might be most satisfying, all in a way that honors and flows out of the unique person(s) that God made you/them to be.

Important points to remember

1. God created each of us with our unique inclinations and preferences; our diversity is a manifestation of how amazing He is.

2. None of the attributes listed are negative or superior or inferior; all of them have potential strengths, blind spots, and challenges. You can find saints with each of these attributes.

3. Most of us will likely have attributes that fall into multiple clusters, and that's okay. Read any/all of the cluster descriptions that you think best describe this person, and use the information that is most helpful.

4. All of us change over time; what we prefer right now might not be what we prefer forever. And as we grow, we'll learn to value every aspect of God. These clusters don't define us, they are simply meant to help us recognize how God made each of us to hunger for Him, and how He wants to satisfy, nourish, and grow us into who He made us to be.

A note on age and developmental stages in children and youth

While each of our personal inclinations likely leads us to hunger after God in a particular way, another factor that we need to be aware of is child and adolescent development.[17] Children at different stages of development tend to hunger for God in different ways, and they also need us to be using different, age-appropriate methods of helping them to encounter Him. The flavor of the encounter and the method we use to offer it changes over time as they grow and develop.[18]

We have an appendix to help you see how children at certain stages of development tend to hunger for God and how parents and adults who love them can walk with them through those years of their journey. This may be especially helpful to parents of younger children (approximately age 7 or younger) who are beginning to reveal their personalities and preferences, but who are also growing and changing so rapidly that it may be difficult to pinpoint anything specific and consistent just yet.[19]

V(C). Use the Instrument: Understand Your Craving

Genesis 13:16

"You are the God who sees me."

The following exercise can be used to better see and know your children, or even yourself. Children around age 10 and older can complete the exercise for themselves, and then discuss and compare their own answers with those of their parents, family members, or ministry leaders. You can use this instrument again and again, for as many individuals as you'd like.

The attributes you choose should be traits that describe who this person is, not just how you or they act. For example, many of us can be helpful, but only some of us have a true personality that thrives on being helpful and seeks and recognizes such opportunities daily.

Circle or highlight the attributes that most describe yourself or your child...

- Active • Adventurous • Affectionate • Ambitious • Artistic

- Analytical • Assertive • Compassionate • Competitive

- Cooperative • Creative • Curious • Easy-going • Experimental

- Expressive • Happy • Helpful • Imaginative • Leader • Logical

- Makes friends easily • Optimistic • Orderly • Organized • Outgoing

- Peacemaker • Pragmatic • Private • Quiet • Reflective

- Spontaneous • Talkative • Values alone time • Values routines

Pick 3-4 of the adjectives that you have selected that you think are your *most* prominent attributes (or your child's *most* prominent):

1. _____

2. _____

3. _____

4. _____

*If you are using this instrument with older children, have them self-evaluate while you list the attributes that you see in them separately. Sit down together and talk about similarities or differences that you had in your answers. This is a great time to affirm your children's unique gifts, but also for you to understand how they see themselves. Think of a memory that shows your children embodying the most typical adjectives you chose and share that with them.

Now what?

On the following pages, you'll find which flavor—***Beauty, Truth, or Goodness***—individuals with each attribute are most likely craving.

You'll also find that we offer spiritual feeding guidance based on the age and stage that children and youth might be in.

To really personalize this process, we need to take ***both*** of those into consideration: ***what*** our children are craving (flavor), and ***how*** we feed it to them (feeding guidance). Because both matter, we offer two different appendices so you can explore how to help your particular children, whatever their craving and whatever their age.

The "Flavors and Attribute Clusters" chart on p. 34 will show you which flavor(s) and cluster(s) your own and your children's attributes fall into. You can explore more nuanced, practical guidance for each cluster in Appendix A.

The "Ages and Feeding Methods" chart on p. 35 will show you a method for feeding children and youth at different stages. You can explore more nuanced, practical guidance on how to offer spiritual nourishment each age and stage in Appendix B.

Of course, feel free to read the descriptions of clusters that don't contain any of your attributes, as well as guidance for ages that aren't in your current lived reality. If those suggestions feel more helpful, then use them! The goal is not to box ourselves in; it is to help us recognize patterns in the way our children's built-in hunger for God manifests, and to know how best to offer them an encounter with Him so that they can experience the satisfaction that only He can give.

Psalm 139:1-3

"You have searched me, Lord, and you know me. You know when I sit and when I rise; you perceive my thoughts from afar. You discern my going out and my lying down; you are familiar with all my ways."

"**One** who **knows** **oneself** knows **God.** Therefore, my **beloveds** in the **Lord,** know **yourselves."**

St. Anthony the Great

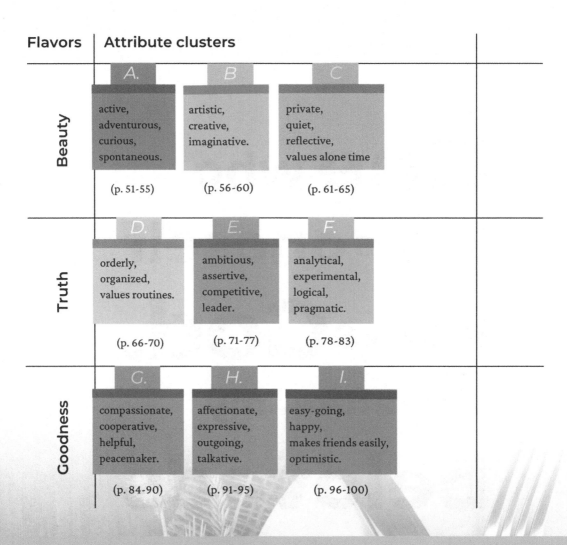

Flavors | **Attribute clusters**

	A.	B.	C.
Beauty	active, adventurous, curious, spontaneous.	artistic, creative, imaginative.	private, quiet, reflective, values alone time
	(p. 51-55)	(p. 56-60)	(p. 61-65)
	D.	E.	F.
Truth	orderly, organized, values routines.	ambitious, assertive, competitive, leader.	analytical, experimental, logical, pragmatic.
	(p. 66-70)	(p. 71-77)	(p. 78-83)
	G.	H.	I.
Goodness	compassionate, cooperative, helpful, peacemaker.	affectionate, expressive, outgoing, talkative.	easy-going, happy, makes friends easily, optimistic.
	(p. 84-90)	(p. 91-95)	(p. 96-100)

To start exploring the flavor preferences and practical guidance for individuals with these attributes, go to Appendix A (p. 48).

Or you can read the next page to learn about feeding your children through their developmental stages.

V(D). Feeding Through Developmental Stages

Each person is unique in all the world, but developmentally, we need to see how our children likely need to be fed and offered nourishment differently in different ages and stages.

In addition to specific guidance based on each of their attributes and inclinations, we can use these developmentally appropriate flavor preferences and feeding methods to help them encounter the Lord in a way that is particularly satisfying.

It's not just what we offer, but how we offer it that matters.

Ages	Feeding methods
Up to 7 years old (p. 103-105)	We need to be doing much of the work of feeding for our children at this stage, similar to spoon-feeding or "follow the leader" style.
8-13 years old (p. 106-108)	At this stage, we need to invite them to come alongside us, shoulder-to-shoulder, as we show them how and why to eat.
Teenagers & young adults (p. 109-112)	We need to empower and support them as they grow into independent eaters, motivated to eat and even feed others, because they see the difference it makes.

Dr. John Trainer

"Children are not a distraction from more important work. They are the most important work."

For further guidance on feeding your children through developmental stages, go to Appendix B (p. 102).

Or to explore practical guidance for flavor preferences and the different attribute clusters, go to Appendix A (p. 48).

Chapter VI. Becoming Food for the World

John 15:4-5

Watch Now!

https://ablz.org/tobt-videos

"Remain in me, as I also remain in you. No branch can bear fruit by itself; it must remain in the vine. Neither can you bear fruit unless you remain in me. I am the vine; you are the branches. If you remain in me and I in you, you will bear much fruit; apart from me you can do nothing."

In the previous chapters and in *the One Best Thing Instrument*, we've been looking at how we were created to hunger for the Lord, and how each of us can encounter and be fed by Him. Within each trait cluster segment, we started to look at how each of us can share God's nourishing, satisfying love with others too.

Now we'll look at a process to help each of us (ourselves and our children) discern where it is that the Lord might want to be at work in and through us to change the world, allowing us to be part of the way He feeds others.

Becoming food for the world

1. Encounter the Lord personally as He comes to you in the Sacraments, the Church, prayer, Scripture, community, creation, and everyday life.

2. Allow His love to nourish and satisfy you, which will allow you to grow more and more into who He created you to be throughout your life.

3. Ask the Holy Spirit to guide you. How is He calling and empowering you to participate in God's great work of salvation, to live out the purpose of your unique and unrepeatable life?

The truth that perhaps many of us don't know or fully believe is this:

There is good in each of us, and the Lord put it there. He loves us, and He will grow the good in us and use it for even greater good if we let Him. In fact, it's been part of His plan from the beginning, but we can't do it without Him.

As we encounter and respond to the Lord, our own satisfaction and joy not only becomes even more substantial, it spreads. Our encounters with Him aren't meant to be kept to ourselves; they're meant to transform us into a gift to the world.

This might seem counterintuitive, especially in a world that so often tries to convince us that easy, comfortable, successful lives lead to the greatest satisfaction. But all we have to do is pick any saint and see how encountering, responding to, and sharing God's love was what actually changed each of their lives for the better.

Pope St. John Paul II, *Gaudium et Spes*

"Man cannot fully find himself except through a sincere gift of himself." [20]

Pope Benedict XVI

"The world will offer you comfort. But you were not made for comfort; you were made for greatness."

So the question is not *if* God wants to be at work in and through us to help others to experience the satisfaction that He brings; the question is *how*. How has the Lord created you to participate in His great work of salvation?

It doesn't have to be a mystery. We can look for patterns in the way God has been at work in our own lives, and how the Holy Spirit is guiding us right here and now.

Key areas that we'll look at

1. **The life you're already living.** Sometimes we think that God calls people to go to far away lands and feed the world there. While that is sometimes true, it's more often the case that He has a mission for us right where we are, in the life we are already living.

2. **Intentional acts of service.** It's important to allow love to flow freely out of us by serving others in our daily lives, as opportunities arise. But it's also important to carve out time to serve others.

First, in the life that you are already living: it's highly likely that the Lord wants to be at work in and through you right where you are. Pay attention to those gentle nudges He gives you: the feeling that you ought to do something, the idea that keeps coming up, etc. Those nudges, recurring thoughts, and opportunities for good are often promptings from the Holy Spirit.

Give your children space to reflect upon and share the nudges they receive too.

Reflection: the life you're already living

- Where has the Lord placed you?
    - Who are the people and what are the situations already in your life?
    - How might the Lord be calling you to help nourish people there with His love?

- When have you ever felt the feeling that you ought to do something, or had the idea that keeps coming up, or seen the person whose need is obvious to you? Those nudges, recurring thoughts, and opportunities for good are often promptings from the Holy Spirit.

- Is there a saint/Scripture that inspires you? Do you see the Lord at work in any situation in your life that is similar to that saint/Scripture?

- What consistently makes you feel alive?
    - The Lord doesn't always work in and through our feelings, but He doesn't avoid them either. There is a certain feeling that often comes when the Spirit is at work within us that can be described as feeling "fully alive," like a light is shining within you. It's a light that isn't your own, but it cooperates with and builds on your own. Have you experienced this? What were you doing when you felt it?

- What do those who know and love you best say about you?
    - What patterns do they recognize in your life and in the way you consistently bring goodness to the world?

Note: we always have to be careful about over-valuing other people's opinions. That doesn't mean we shouldn't value them at all though, especially when it comes to the people who know, love, and care about us most, since the Lord might be working through them to speak to us.

St. Ignatius Loyola

"Whatever you are doing, that which makes you feel most alive...that is where God is."

Intentional Acts of Service: it's also important and good to seek out specific opportunities to serve in ways that stretch us and put us in direct contact with people in need. Love is a choice and needs to be put into action. As you discern where to spend your time in loving service to others, consider this:

Reflection: preparing to intentionally serve others

- What consistently moves you?
  - What sort of injustice, suffering, or need do you observe in the world that upsets you? Which populations and their situations do you want to do something about?

- What opportunities exist in your community?

- What unique gifts or passions do you bring to the world? Remember that "gifts" aren't just abilities according to worldly standards. Your sense of humor, willingness to listen, ability to notice others, etc. have been given to you by God in order to be shared.

St. Francis de Sales

"There is nothing small in the service of God."

Reflection after serving

- How did that experience make you feel?
  - Service might not always feel good, but what God is calling you to do shouldn't feel like drudgery either, at least not all the time.

*Remember: not every good work is **your** work to do. The Lord has a specific role for you to play in **His** plan of salvation. It's okay to serve in some way and discern that this is not what the Lord is calling you to do.*

- How did that experience allow you to grow?
  - Did this opportunity invite you to become more authentically yourself?
  - Did it seem like the Lord was inviting you to stretch?
  - What do you have that these people need?

Remember, Jesus says the same thing to us as He said to His disciples in Luke 11:9-10:

Luke 11:9-10

"So I say to you: Ask and it will be given to you; seek and you will find; knock and the door will be opened to you. For the one who seeks finds; and to the one who knocks, the door will be opened."

If we ask Him in prayer, seek Him in truth, and knock on the door of opportunities, He will answer and show us His plan for us. He said it, and He will do it.

Notes, Thoughts, and Reflections

Chapter VII. Personalizing This Process

St. Padre Pio

"In the spiritual life, he who does not advance goes backward. It happens as with a boat which always must go ahead. If it stands still the wind will blow it back."

The Lord calls *us* to be part of the feeding therapy process for our children.

Each "piece" in spiritual feeding therapy is necessary, part of a process that plays out over time. The Lord is so very patient, revealing Himself gradually. So we need to be patient too.

Maybe some of these pieces are already in place, and that's wonderful! But none of us is ever fully finished going through spiritual feeding therapy and being part of it for others, since free will, concupiscence (our tendency to be attracted to sin), and ever-growing minds and hearts mean that we will need this all the way to eternity.

We need to remember that *the One Best Thing* is ultimately what God wants most; it is *His* plan that we would encounter Him, respond to Him, grow and be nourished by Him, share Him with others, and experience life to the full. *He* is the great mover and power behind everything, including our own desire to be fed and to help others be fed.

Like the crust of a pie, it is God's love that holds the spiritual feeding therapy process together and gives it power to transform lives.

Spiritual feeding therapy is a personalized process, and we need to prayerfully consider what *our* next right step is. Take a look at each piece of the plan on the following pages, and prayerfully identify how well each aspect is already happening. Then, prayerfully discern which one of those areas should be your focus right now.

Matthew 5:6

"Blessed are those who hunger and thirst for righteousness, for they shall be satisfied."

Remember: this is a process. Ask the Lord to help you see clearly what most needs your attention first.

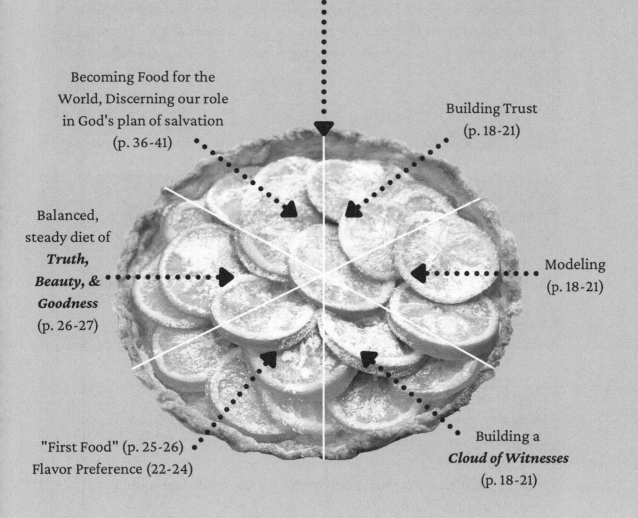

Like the crust, God's power, presence, and love surrounds and supports every piece of pie. *The One Best Thing* is what *He* wants most, and He alone can make it happen. We need to cooperate with and trust Him as we actively participate in His plan.

Becoming Food for the World, Discerning our role in God's plan of salvation (p. 36-41)

Building Trust (p. 18-21)

Balanced, steady diet of *Truth, Beauty, & Goodness* (p. 26-27)

Modeling (p. 18-21)

"First Food" (p. 25-26) Flavor Preference (22-24)

Building a *Cloud of Witnesses* (p. 18-21)

On top of everything, we can't overlook the importance of *joy*. Like powdered sugar sprinkled on top of the pie, joy makes this process sweet for all of us.

Joy is a fruit that the Holy Spirit wants to bear in and through our lives. Do you feel like you don't have it? Ask Him to come more deeply into your own life and bear the fruit of joy, sprinkling it over every aspect of your life and every effort you make.

Reflection

- On a scale of 1-10, *1 being "not at all" and 10 being "very,"* how strong are each of the following pieces of spiritual feeding therapy currently?

BUILDING TRUST

Establishing the kind of relationship with your children that allows them to trust you and know that you love them, making them willing to let you guide them in faith and invite them into an encounter (or repeated encounter) with the Lord.

1   2   3   4   5   6   7   8   9   1 0

MODELING

Living by example *and* by explanation so that they can see and believe that Jesus and His Church make an actual, wonderful difference in all of our lives. Taking time to be with Him in prayer; admitting when we're wrong or when we just don't know something; and seeking and giving mercy generously.

1   2   3   4   5   6   7   8   9   1 0

CLOUD OF WITNESSES

Having a community who also desires *the One Best Thing* that can support and accompany us, modeling faith for one another, and our kids.

Seeking out friends for your children who are also encountering and responding to the Lord.

Surrounding them with adults who are spiritually invested in their lives, and who can become trusted mentors in the faith.

1   2   3   4   5   6   7   8   9   1 0

FLAVOR PREFERENCE/"FIRST FOOD"

This is the "gateway" to encounter. The instrument helps to identify this by recognizing patterns in what a person is primarily attracted and drawn to *Beauty, Truth, or Goodness*. This helps us to know how individuals are most likely to encounter the Lord in a satisfying way so that they'll know firsthand the difference He makes, and want to keep encountering and responding to Him.

1	2	3	4	5	6	7	8	9	10

BALANCED, SUSTAINED DIET OF TRUTH, BEAUTY, AND GOODNESS

Once each of us has an authentic encounter with the Lord (usually by way of our flavor preference), that can and should be leveraged to start introducing more ways to encounter and respond to Him, making sure that we end up being exposed to lots of *Beauty, Truth, and Goodness* over and over and over (and not *just* our favorite flavor).

1	2	3	4	5	6	7	8	9	10

BECOMING FOOD FOR THE WORLD/DISCERNING OUR ROLE IN GOD'S PLAN OF SALVATION

Each of us was made on purpose, with a purpose, and part of our unique purpose is to play a particular role in God's plan for saving the world. Our role includes helping others prayerfully discern how the Lord is calling them, often through something they're passionate about and often related to their own particular flavor preference/craving.

1	2	3	4	5	6	7	8	9	10

It's possible that many or all of these areas could use some work, and that's okay. Don't be discouraged or overwhelmed! Focus on one step at a time; that's how feeding therapy works.

Isaiah 41:10

"So do not fear, for I am with you; do not be dismayed, for I am your God. I will strengthen you and help you; I will uphold you with my righteous right hand."

It is the Holy Spirit, first poured out on each of us at Baptism, Who guides and empowers us. He is very much at work in this whole process.

So ask Him: what is the next best step? There might be many ideas that you like from this book and that you'll eventually use. But which one should you start with? The Holy Spirit knows. Ask Him.

Where to Start: Ask the Holy Spirit

- Which piece of the spiritual feeding therapy process do you feel called to work on right now?

- What support, resource, or opportunity do you need to strengthen and encourage you in this? Who might be able to help with this?

- These six aspects of spiritual feeding therapy aren't exhaustive. Has the Spirit brought anything else to your attention that could help others encounter and respond to Him?

Since the beginning of time, the Lord has called people (and parents, specifically) to partner with Him in drawing His beloved children to Himself, to do the work of spiritual feeding therapy. Do not be afraid. You were born for this!

Deuteronomy 6:4-9

"Hear, O Israel: The Lord our God, the Lord is one. Love the Lord your God with all your heart and with all your soul and with all your strength. These commandments that I give you today are to be on your hearts. Impress them on your children. Talk about them when you sit at home and when you walk along the road, when you lie down and when you get up. Tie them as symbols on your hands and bind them on your foreheads. Write them on the doorframes of your houses and on your gates."

Notes, Thoughts, and Reflections

Appendix A

Attribute Guide

I. Navigate the Resources

Appendix A: Preference Guide

1. **A description of individuals in that cluster,** how they are likely to be craving God—primarily through *Beauty, Truth, or Goodness*—and how those cravings might manifest for them in a particular way.

2. **Suggestions for how to help these individuals truly encounter the Lord in a way that satisfies and brings joy,** not just to learn about Him (though that's also important). Like St. Augustine described his own experience in his "Confessions," the Lord is trying to get our attention in a personal way.

3. **Prayer suggestions.** Our relationship with the Lord requires an initial encounter and sustained, recurring encounters with Him in big or small ways. Learning to pray in a way that fits our inclination helps us recognize and respond to Him personally.

4. **Potential prayer and spiritual blind spots or challenges that these people might encounter.** Everyone has them, but there are ways to help navigate them.

5. **Ways that God can be at work in and through these individuals to draw others to Himself.**

6. **Scripture passages and saints that might be particularly encouraging for individuals with these attributes.** All of the saints listed had these attributes, and every attribute has the potential for holiness. Consider printing one of these each week/month and displaying them in your home.

After the attribute clusters, there is Appendix C called "Encountering the Lord in the Everyday" (p. 114). Here, you'll find practical ways that you and your children can recognize and encounter the Lord in the life you are already living—through the Sacraments and intentional prayer, literature, the five senses, nature, family activities and traditions, service, media, and sports/competition.

In the "Encountering the Lord Through Prayer and the Sacraments" chapter (p. 116-126), we help to break down different ways that you can pray together, while still helping each person pursue God and be pursued by Him, in the way that is likely to be most satisfying. Because any true encounter with God will always be an encounter with **Beauty, Truth, and Goodness** (because that's Who He is), prayer can be approached from any one of those inclinations, even if one seems more obvious than the others.

Note: *For more in depth, practical guidance on how to use and practice some of the forms of prayer mentioned in the "Encountering God Through Prayer and the Sacraments" chapter, see our downloadable prayer guide!* ablazefamily.org/obt-prayer-guide/

A. Attributes: Active, adventurous, curious, spontaneous.

Individuals who are active, adventurous, curious, or spontaneous are likely to be primarily craving *Beauty*, particularly as it manifests in creation around them. They want to do more than observe and appreciate beauty; they want to be part of it!

They are most likely to encounter the Lord outdoors, in activity, while using their bodies during prayer, or in new ways. Seeing all of creation as a sign and symbol of God's love and presence will likely help these individuals to not only appreciate God, but to personally welcome Him more fully into their own life.

The Holy Spirit can help these individuals with all of this, and enhance and enliven their already adventurous spirit with His gifts of wonder, awe, and reverence: the ability to marvel at all that God has made and honor Him for it all.

"To fall in love with God is the greatest romance; to seek him the greatest adventure; to find him, the greatest human achievement."

They might benefit from praying like this...

- **Active, hands-on opportunities/experiences:** doodling/coloring while praying, walking while praying the rosary, reflecting, or praying the stations of the cross, praying while hiking/being active outdoors, etc.

- **Praise and worship and charismatic, spontaneous, and imaginative prayer** where they learn to meditate on and "enter in" to a Bible story.

- **Taking pilgrimages, going on active retreats, participating in Catholic adventure camps, serving others, and going on adventures with others.**

- **Learning Theology of the Body,** seeing how God made their bodies on purpose, as part of the way He shows His love to them (and to all of us) and part of the way we all can respond in love to Him and to others.

Scan QR code for more prayer guidance

ablazefamily.org/obt-prayer-guide/

Potential prayer/spiritual blind spots or challenges...

- **Seeing that each adventure can be a prayer and that we can intentionally welcome the Lord to show us His glory as we hike, play, run, bike, etc.**
  - **How parents and parish ministers can help:**
    - Model this for them so they can learn to always be in "treasure hunt mode," looking for and finding God's treasures and manifestations of love, power, presence, and faithfulness everywhere. Ask them every day where they saw God at work, and ask what things God might be working through in the world around them to get their attention.
    - Acknowledge any moment when you are able to see how the beauty around you points back to the Creator. Thank Him for it right then and there, and acknowledge that He created it with you and this exact moment in mind (Psalm 139:2).

- **Learning to pause long enough to reflect before moving on to the next adventure, since much of what we experience is only fully experienced when we can pause and give it time to sink in.**
  - How parents and parish ministers can help:
    - During your adventure time and meal-time conversations, build in time to reflect and share favorite moments and biggest lessons, so that they learn to reflect and share.

- **Seeing discipleship as a life-long adventure, which has many ups, downs, twists, and turns, but is also where the Lord is our constant companion and guide.**
  - How parents and parish ministers can help:
    - Introduce them to adventurous saints who had moments of great joy and great struggle, so that they can help model what this looks like in an ever-growing relationship with the Lord.

- **Developing a habit of prayer, as opposed to waiting to be inspired to pray.** It's important to realize that cultivating a daily habit of prayer invites the Holy Spirit to be part of our lives more fully. He gives us "eyes" to see God at work in all things, which is a great adventure!
  - How parents and parish ministers can help:
    - Invite these individuals into a family or group prayer routine, have them share insight, and thank them for it. It will help affirm their insight, even in times of prayer that didn't grow out of inspiration so much as routine.
    - Model for them how to ask the Holy Spirit to give you the courage you need to commit to praying consistently, even when it feels hard. With His help, we can do hard things.

- **Learning to cultivate silence.** Everyone benefits from intentional times of silence and internal stillness, and they will likely need to be more intentional about it since they're not drawn to it naturally.
  - How parents and parish ministers can help:
    - Assure them that if silence makes them feel uncomfortable, then they can start small! Carve out 3-5 minutes to start.

Encourage them to tell the Lord everything on their mind and in their heart, give it to Him, and then be still and allow Him to be God of it all. It might feel like they're doing nothing at first, but when we practice being silent, we come to discover that we're actually giving God more room to do things in and through us.

- Encourage these individuals to gradually increase the amount of time they spend in silence each day.
- Silence can happen anywhere; at home, outdoors, in a church. Because of our Baptism, the Lord lives inside of each of us. So with a little practice, all of us can learn to listen to Him and be attentive to Him anywhere.

They can respond to and share the Lord with others by...

- **Helping others develop "eyes that see";** the ability to recognize the God's fingerprint all over creation and be energized by it is a gift that probably comes more easily to these individuals than to others. They can share what they're experiencing through wonder and awe.

- **Accompanying others as companions for the journey; none of us are meant to go through discipleship alone.**

- **Helping to keep momentum, energy, and positivity to stay the course, for themselves and others.**

Do you want to explore a different cluster? Just head back to p. 34 to find the master list of all cluster options and their pages.

Or are you ready to move on to the next step in the process? Go to p. 36 to start "Becoming Food for the World."

Psalm 84: 5

"Blessed are those whose strength is in you, whose hearts are set on pilgrimage."

Scriptures and saints that might be particularly relatable and relevant

Exodus 14:14, 15:3	Bl. Chiara Badano
1 Samuel 17 (especially verse 45)	Pope St. John Paul II
Psalm 23:6, 46:11, 84:5	St. Augustine
Proverbs 3:5-6	St. Brendan
Lamentations 3:22-23	St. Damien of Molokai
Matthew 14:22-33 Matthew 28:20	St. Francis Xavier
	St. Josephine Bakhita
	St. Marianne Cope
	Sts. Paul and Peter
	St. Pier Giorgio Frassati
	St. Rose Philippine Duchesne
	St. Teresa of Calcutta
	Venerable Michael McGivney

St. Bernard of Clarivaux

"What I know of the divine sciences and the Holy Scriptures, I have learned in woods and fields. I have no other masters than the beeches and the oaks."

St. Josephine Bakhita

Josephine was kidnapped from her family in Africa and sold into slavery. Her life was full of suffering that might make someone else bitter, but Josephine had a hungry sense of wonder that couldn't be stifled. This opened her heart to encountering God, even though she had never even heard of Christianity yet. He came to her through the beauty of nature, and she said this:

"Seeing the sun, the moon, and the stars, I said to myself, 'Who could be the Master of these beautiful things?' I felt a great desire to see him, to know him, and to pay him homage."[1]

B. Attributes: Artistic, creative, imaginative.

These individuals are likely to be primarily craving **Beauty**, particularly as it manifests in ways that they can see, hear, taste, touch, and smell things like literature, art, music and sound, stories and poetry, food, scented candles and essential oils, etc. Our imagination is often considered the sixth sense, which can be another way they may be inspired to encounter the Lord.

They are most likely to encounter the Lord through their senses and experiences that engage their imagination: art, music, theater, stories, film, dance, etc.

The Holy Spirit can help these individuals by pouring out His gifts of wonder, awe, and reverence, helping them recognize the beauty in feast days, liturgical celebrations, and symbols in the Church. If they ask for and welcome His help, they will start to see that everything beautiful is but a glimpse of the Beautiful One, our God who is beautiful beyond imagining. All of it points back to Him. And humans, point back to the Beauty of God in a particular way, because we are made in His image and likeness.

Pope St. John Paul II, *Letter to Artists*, 1999

"...'beauty will save the world'...Artists of the world, may your many different paths all lead to that infinite Ocean of beauty where wonder becomes awe, exhilaration, unspeakable joy."

They might benefit from praying like this...

- **Engaging their imagination and their senses in prayer** by lighting candles, using sacred art or sacred music, reading saint and Scripture stories aloud, and allowing and encouraging them to really "enter in" to that prayer.

- **Lectio Divina (Latin for "holy reading," a way of reading Scripture), Visio Divina (Latin for "holy looking," a way of using art to pray), and using their imaginations to meditate** on the mysteries of the rosary and Scripture.

- **Going to Eucharistic Adoration will likely be most fruitful if they have something beautiful to ponder and a way to process their thoughts creatively** through journaling, doodling, meditations and reflections, etc.

- **Reminding themselves of the truth that the Lord is always with us,** so they can converse with Him constantly in the silence of their hearts.

- **Praying outside in places that are beautiful and inspiring.**

- **Seeking mentors who are like themselves** (mentors who are alive now *and* the saints) who can help "train" them to use their natural love and appreciation for beauty to be able to easily love and appreciate spiritual beauty too.

- **Practicing welcoming the Holy Spirit, who prompts, guides, and inspires them (and all of us) toward *Beauty, Truth, and Goodness*.** Learning to listen to Him in the silence of their hearts will awaken their awareness of and desire for beauty all the more. It's okay if it takes some time for them to learn how to recognize the Holy Spirit in the silence.

Scan QR code for more prayer guidance

ablazefamily.org/obt-prayer-guide/

- **They might have a hard time appreciating rote prayer, rhythm and repetition in the liturgy, and a routine of prayer.**
  - **How parents and ministers can help:**
    - Let them discover the goodness of routine and rhythm by pointing out the routine, rhythm, and patterns in the beauty (music, art, nature, etc.) all around us. Help connect the dots so that they see how structure allows for great freedom and even more beauty.

- **Individuals with these attributes might not initially see the full value of truth or goodness, particularly if they seem separated from or hampering to beauty.** The 10 Commandments, precepts of the Church, teachings on human sexuality and morality, Catholic Social Teaching—all of this might seem irrelevant or even in conflict to beauty for these individuals.
  - **How parents and ministers can help:**
    - Help them find a saint who was also artistic or creative and was able to embrace goodness and truth. Help them befriend the saints in this way, which allows for the saints to inspire and "call them on" in a way that feels encouraging, instead of condemning.
    - Ask them to identify what is beautiful about God and what He has made. Ask them how this beauty is connected to to truth (something that is consistently real) and goodness (the beauty is related in some way to how God is good to us).
    - Don't be afraid to allow them to wrestle or struggle in this area of faith. Share insight, the wisdom of the Church as passed down through the ages, and help them find a faithful mentor and guide (youth minister, small group leader, spiritual advisor, coach, etc.) who can also accompany them as they navigate their questions.
    - Pray with and for them for the gift of understanding, that the Lord will do the hard work of opening our eyes to truth and goodness if we have trouble seeing.

- **Creating objects/experiences that others can see, touch, taste, hear, smell, and ponder,** so they can experience God's Beauty too.

- **Sharing their own thoughts and reflections.** Because these individuals have a natural eye for beauty and that can translate into having a spiritual eye for beauty, their ponderings and prayerful insights can help others see and recognize beauty more easily than they might be able to do by themselves.

- **Helping others to find beauty in secular art,** and using it as a way to draw others into the Beauty that is the Lord.

- **Helping to create an environment of incarnational beauty:** beautiful spaces and experiences that can help lead others to an experience of being and feeling loved.

Do you want to explore a different cluster? Just head back to p. 34 to find the master list of all cluster options and their pages.

Or are you ready to move on to the next step in the process? Go to p. 36 to start "Becoming Food for the World."

Psalm 139:14

"I praise you because I am fearfully and wonderfully made; your works are wonderful, I know that full well."

Scriptures and saints that might be particularly relatable and relevant

Genesis 1:1	Bl. Fra Angelico
Genesis 1:27	Bl. Fructuoso Perez Marquez
Exodus 35:35	Bl. Maria Dina Belanger
Psalm 100: 1-5	Pope St. John Paul II

Scriptures and saints (continued)

Psalm 104: 24	St. Albert Chmielowski
Psalm 139: 13-15	St. Catherine of Bologna
Jeremiah 1:5	St. Cecilia
Jeremiah 10:12	St. Gregory I
Matthew 25: 14-30	St. Hildegard of Bingen
Romans 1:2 & 6	St. Luke
Ephesians 2:10	St. Nicetas of Remesiana
Colossians 3:23	St. Romanus the Melodist

Bl. Fra Angelico

His nickname, "Fra Angelico" means "angelic friar." It was given to him by his brother Dominicans, because everyone could see that he really was holy. His paintings were and are famous, and over time he received requests from the most wealthy and "important" people in Europe. But Fra Angelico didn't let that go to his head; he knew where his talent came from. Before he ever worked on one of his artworks, he spent hours and hours in prayer. He knew that to be able to paint something beautiful, he needed to spend time with the One who is Beauty itself. [3]

C. Attributes: Private, quiet, reflective, values alone time.

These individuals are likely to be primarily craving **Beauty**, particularly as it manifests in the tranquility, renewal, and clarity that they experience from time spent pondering.

They are likely to encounter the Lord during time and space carved out for silence. They benefit from remembering that Jesus often withdrew to pray and be with His Father; that intimate time with the Lord recharged and empowered Jesus, and it will do the same for them.

The Holy Spirit can help transform their already present appreciation for silence and peace into a holy and powerful encounter, through His gifts of wonder, awe, and reverence.

"Silence is God's first language."

They might benefit from praying like this...

- **Through quiet reflection; time in Eucharistic Adoration; meditation; and prayerfully reading spiritual books, stories of the saints, and devotionals.**

- **Meditating and praying in ways that allow for a slower pace:** the rosary, Divine Mercy chaplet, Lectio Divina (Latin for "holy reading," a way of praying with Scripture), etc.

- **Participating in liturgies with built-in times of silence that allow for more of a response in their heart.**

- **Remembering that their hearts (and all of our hearts) are a place where God dwells with us always, waiting to meet us in the quiet and stillness.** This helps their alone time to not truly be alone. But rather, it is time spent with the One who loves them most (even, or perhaps especially, in the silence).

- **Finding people throughout history and Scripture (like Hannah, Joseph, and Simeon) who were "in the background," but still played a pivotal role.** God had big plans for all of them, even when His plan didn't look "big," loud, or important. The seemingly small, insignificant things are pivotal too, and the Lord works in and through all of that. The Holy Family is a great example of this, quietly living their lives and sharing their love with each other and the world.

Scan QR code for more prayer guidance

ablazefamily.org/obt-prayer-guide/

Potential prayer/spiritual blind spots or challenges...

- **Becoming annoyed or impatient with those who are less pensive, louder, or more interested in being with others.**
  - **How parents and parish ministers can help:**
    - Help them find louder, less pensive saints. This will help them see that

God loves these individuals too and that they bring something valuable to the Church, the world, and even our ponderers.

- **Seeing that God is also with them "when two or more are gathered in His name" and that we all need community.** We grow by being surrounded by faithful people, and we help them grow too. It doesn't have to be a huge crowd or involve more expressive types of prayer.
  - **How parents and parish ministers can help:**
    - Help them cultivate a friendship or two within larger communities like youth group/bible study so that they always feel like they have a "wingman," as opposed to feeling like they have to participate equally with everyone in the group.
    - Enlist the help of parish leaders and your *cloud of witnesses* here! Invite others to join you in calling your child by name and engaging them, all while respecting their potential preference to not engage in larger, more lively groups.

- **Recognizing that while they might not always be called to stand on a stage or command a large group, they are still called to something meaningful and important.**
  - **How parents and parish ministers can help:**
    - Remind them that God has no favorites or least favorites, "understudies," or "third string team." All of us and each of us are part of God's great story of salvation.

- **Mistakenly thinking that service is necessarily a "peopley" experience and avoiding it because they prefer quieter time.**
  - **How parents and parish ministers can help:**
    - Help these individuals recognize "behind the scenes" people who serve in your own parish and community, and find similar ways to serve. Help them practice gratitude to start seeing the cycle of goodness that the Lord invites us into; we can be generous, even quietly and anonymously, as many others have been to us. In this way, we share in God's gift of Goodness to others.

- **Being a good listener and recognizing that, while it might feel like a sacrifice, it is a tremendous gift to others.**

- **Bringing others' needs to the Lord:** asking others how they can pray for them and intentionally setting aside time to do so.

- **Writing down insights that they receive during prayer and sharing it with others.** They are likely capable of a depth in prayer that some might have never experienced, and they can share that with others.

Do you want to explore a different cluster? Just head back to p. 34 to find the master list of all cluster options and their pages.

Or are you ready to move on to the next step in the process? Go to p. 36 to start "Becoming Food for the World."

Mark 1:35

"Very early in the morning, while it was still dark, Jesus got up, left the house and went off to a solitary place, where he prayed."

Scriptures and saints that might be particularly relatable and relevant

Exodus 14:14	St. Anthony the Great
Job 6:24	St. Benedict of Nursia
Psalm 30: 4-5, 46: 10, 62:5, 139:7-12	St. Bernadette
Isaiah 32:17	St. Clare
Matthew 14:23	St. Faustina
Mark 1:35	St. John of the Cross
Luke 2:19, 2:33, 2:51, 5:15-16	St. Joseph and Mother Mary
John 14: 27	St. Margaret Mary Alacoque
Romans 15:13	St. Mary Magdalene
2 Timothy 1:7	St. Moses the Black
James 1:2	St. Paul of Thebes

Saints (continued)

St. Joseph

St. Joseph was chosen to be Jesus' earthly father. He and Mary loved, raised, and helped Jesus. It's likely that nobody on earth loved Jesus in the same way Joseph did, and nobody on earth was loved by Jesus in the same way Joseph was. He had one of the most important jobs in all of salvation history, and yet we don't know a single word that Joseph actually said! There is nothing recorded in Scripture.

We don't have to be loud to make an impact. While our words are important, the way we live our lives is even more so.

Serving the mission in the background

"During a visit to the NASA space center in 1962, President John F. Kennedy noticed a janitor carrying a broom. He interrupted his tour, walked over to the man and said, 'Hi, I'm Jack Kennedy. What are you doing?'

'Well, Mr. President,' the janitor responded, 'I'm helping put a man on the moon.'

To most people, this janitor was just cleaning the building. But in the larger more mythic, story unfolding around him, he was helping to make history."[4]

D. Attributes: Orderly, organized, values routines.

These individuals are most likely to be primarily craving **Truth**. They appreciate when things are consistent, predictable, and reliable in their environment, and they experience peace and satisfaction when they are rooted in the reality of God's unchanging, consistent and perfect love.

They are most likely to encounter the Lord in quiet ways, in routine or habitual prayer time, and in spending time in mental prayer with the Lord as they notice, appreciate, and ponder the amazing details that He put into creation and all of His works.

They Holy Spirit can make all of this possible, as silence and order allow His gifts of wonder and awe to grow and become stronger in us.

"There is a time for everything, and a season for every activity under the heavens."

They might benefit from praying like this...

- **Developing a habit of making prayer commitments (like novenas or the Liturgy of the Hours) that have a rhythm or schedule.** Also, praying with the Scriptures, especially in the way the Mass readings are broken into a 3-year cycle (years A, B, C), so that we cover all of Scripture over those years.

- **Appreciating and entering into the cycle of the liturgical year and helping to decide how to enter fully into each season/feast.**

- **Coming to appreciate that the predictability and rhythm of the liturgy, Sacraments, and rituals free us to enter into prayer.** They remove uncertainty and guide us with familiarity, so that we can spend our energy on having encounters with the Lord and responding to Him.

- **Studying Scripture in a way that allows them to reflect and experience how the truths of Scripture are still true today.** What the Lord has done in the past is still being done, here and now. He is consistent, reliable, and stable, and we can build our lives upon the Rock that He is.

- **Engaging the teachings of the Church Fathers and the Catechism.**

- **Developing a rhythm or habit of prayer in your life that allows for consistent growth.**

Scan QR code for more prayer guidance

ablazefamily.org/obt-prayer-guide/

Potential prayer/spiritual blind spots or challenges...

- **Tending toward perfectionism in their spiritual life.**
  - **How parents and parish ministers can help:**
    - Help these individuals lower their expectations so they can enjoy praying and spend their energy encountering and responding to the Lord, instead of keeping track of ways that prayer isn't "measuring up" to what they had expected.

- Remind them that God alone is perfect; we can rejoice in the freedom that this gives us. Perfection is the enemy of progress.
- Model forgiveness for them—forgiving oneself and others. It is by grace that we grow, and grace flows through forgiveness.

- **Thinking that God is somehow expecting them to figure things out on their own.**
  - **How parents and parish ministers can help:**
    - Help them by providing them with a *cloud of witnesses*, other people who can speak truth into their lives and model for them how to depend on the Lord and on others. Ask them frequently for help, and ask them how we can help them. Model for them that there's real beauty when we depend on one another and not on ourselves.
    - Go to Reconciliation regularly as a family. Then, do something celebratory after (a trip to the park, a stop for ice cream, etc.). In doing this, you can show them—in a tangible way—that the Lord is not at all expecting us to grow by our own power and strength. He is the source of that power and strength, called grace, and He delights when we return to Him to ask for help!

- **Being tempted to stick to their routines that they actually get into a rut.** These individuals might struggle to appreciate spontaneous prayer, response to inspiration in the moment, or anything else that doesn't come with preparation, warning, or structure.
  - **How parents and parish ministers can help:**
    - Encourage and invite them to try all kinds of new things (not just prayer) and stretch themselves. They will likely respond best to an invitation to join someone else in this, as opposed to being told and expected to do it on their own.
    - Remind these individuals that conversations aren't scripted, so our prayer shouldn't be either. It's good to have a structured prayer life, but we also need to be open to whenever the Lord stands at the door of our heart and knocks (Revelation 3:20), even if we weren't expecting Him.

- Sometimes routines are a manifestation of a desire for control. Model for these individuals a prayer that hands all of our cares and concerns over to the Lord. The Litany of Trust (see prayer guide) might be particularly helpful to add to your routine.

- **Being impatient with those who do not value routines and order as much as they do.**
  - **How parents and parish ministers can help:**
    - Pray for patience; it's a gift that God can give us! Point to examples in nature that reveal how structure and routine interact with and relate to spontaneity or chance to see that both are necessary and good. They need each other.
    - Help them befriend orderly, organized saints. They also had to work on their virtues of patience and kindness!

They can respond to and share the Lord with others by...

- **Helping to establish traditions and routines for family and friends** that provide order in a way that helps them experience stability, peace, and safety.

- **Being a good and patient listener to help others to feel "grounded,"** even if this listening disrupts their schedule and plans.

- **Leading others in/helping them appreciate liturgy or rote prayer.**

- **Encouraging others to develop a prayer habit/schedule and accompany them in that process.**

- **Being good administrators to help keep others on track.**

Do you want to explore a different cluster? Just head back to p. 34 to find the master list of all cluster options and their pages.

Or are you ready to move on to the next step in the process? Go to p. 36 to start "Becoming Food for the World."

"For You formed my inmost being; You knit me together in my mother's womb. I praise You, for I am fearfully and wonderfully made. Marvelous are Your works, and I know this very well."

Scriptures and saints that might be particularly relatable and relevant

Psalm 62:2-3, 121:2, 139:1-3	St. Benedict
Matthew 10:29-31	St. John Vianney
Luke 1:37, 1:45	St. Josemaria Escriva
John 10:10	St. Martha
Colossians 3:1-4	St. Matthew the Evangelist
	St. Scholastica
	St. Teresa of Avila
	St. Thomas Aquinas
	St. Zita

St. Benedict

Benedict was born shortly after the fall of the Roman Empire, a time when chaos, fear, and uncertainty reigned where powerful Emperors had once maintained tight control. It was out of this chaotic time that Benedict emerged, becoming a monk and eventually writing his now famous *Rule of Saint Benedict,* a structured way of living for the monks who lived in the monasteries that he founded. *The Rule* provided balance between prayer, work, and study, because Benedict knew that God could be found and loved in and through each of those, especially if he was intentional about pursuing them in an organized way.

St. Benedict's *Rule* allowed the monks to live organized, structured lives, and as his order spread throughout Europes, their way of life became a source of stability and calm to the villages and world around them for many centuries to come. Benedict helps us see and appreciate the beauty and peace that balance and structure bring.[2]

E. Attributes: Ambitious, assertive, competitive, leader.

These individuals are likely craving *Truth*, particularly as it pertains to discovering and portraying the truth about who they are. They are often people of integrity, passionately striving to live out what they believe to be true. Which is why it is pivotal that they know what is actually true, since they'll be powerfully operating out of it.

They are likely to encounter the Lord in a way that inspires, challenges, and empowers them to grow in virtue and proficiency in some way.

The Holy Spirit's gifts of wisdom, understanding, and knowledge will help them know and believe the truest true thing about who they are: beloved sons and daughters of the Father, loved because He chooses to love them, and not because of anything they've accomplished or achieved.

These individuals tend to have lofty goals and aspirations, which is good; they are ultimately being called to participate in God's plan in a way that nobody else can.

> "As gifts increase in you, let your humility grow, for you must consider that everything is given to you on loan."

They might benefit from praying like this...

- **Encountering the Lord powerfully.** This could come in many different ways: in an inspiring or relevant Scripture passage (like Augustine experienced), in a sense of certainty (an "epiphany" moment) that comes with a powerful teaching, by hearing a powerful testimony, etc. Charismatic prayer, large liturgies, retreats and conferences, and dynamic speakers are likely a good fit.

- **Being connected with a spiritual mentor**, someone who can "coach" and accompany them as they grow.

- **Being encouraged to receive the Eucharist and welcome Jesus to be the powerful One, the great mover in their lives.** They might relate well to Jesus as the One who is powerful, steadfast, committed, and unwavering.

- **Connecting with the glorious mysteries of the rosary,** which demonstrate and invite us into Christ's victory.

- **Reading what St. Paul has to say about running the race and realizing that discipline plays a big role in discipleship.** It's a tangible way to welcome the Lord and pursue Him.

- **Becoming familiar with Scripture passages where Jesus manifested his power and authority:** the miraculous catch of fish (Luke 5:1-11), calming the sea (Mark 4:35-41), turning the tables in the temple (Matthew 21:12-17).

Scan QR code for more prayer guidance

ablazefamily.org/obt-prayer-guide/

Potential prayer/spiritual blind spots or challenges...

- **Recognizing that the Lord also speaks in quieter, simpler ways. Read 1 Kings 19:11-13. God sometimes speaks in a "still, small voice."** If we learn to recognize His voice by practicing listening to it in Scripture, personal prayer, and through the ministry of the Church, then we'll be able to recognize Him whether He whispers or shouts.

- **How parents and parish ministers can help:**
  - Consider hanging this or one of the other Scripture passages listed in this cluster guidance in your home, as a reminder.
  - Carve out time as a family to be silent in prayer. Share with them that, even though silence can feel hard sometimes, or feel like we're just sitting around and doing nothing, it is often in silence and stillness that the Lord can be most at work, even if we don't perceive or feel anything.

- **Realizing that growing in holiness can't be done on their own or by their own strength;** it starts with the Lord, and we respond imperfectly. It is *His* power at work within us that causes change. There are no self-made saints, regardless of how talented or gifted they may be; all talents and gifts are just that—*gifts*! Given by the Powerful One, and not of our own making. Our life-long cooperation is needed.
  - **How parents and parish ministers can help:**
    - These individuals are likely used to being high achievers, and they'll need you to gently keep them in check. No amount of striving makes us holier, but a hefty dose of humility gives the Lord lots of room to be at work.
    - St. Augustine and St. Thomas More are excellent role models for these individuals, demonstrating how to still be high-achievers and live out of our gifting while being humble, docile, and obedient to the Holy Spirit.

- **Potentially being tempted to think that their own identity, dignity, and worth (and potentially that of others) is wrapped up in their own ability to achieve, accomplish, and live up to the truth.** It will be very important to remind them and help them believe that they are good because God made them good. And while we should all try to become the best version of ourselves, our efforts and successes don't make us who we are, and our faults and failures do not "unmake" us who we are. We are created by God and claimed by Him in Baptism, and that is the deepest and most untouchable source of our inherent goodness and dignity.

- **Craving to be powerful or in control to the point of lacking charity for others.**
  - **How parents and parish ministers can help:**
    - Serve together as a family. Model for them that their gifts were given in order to be shared, to be a blessing for others and not just for themselves.
    - Help them recognize and see how their gifts are needed in the family, the community, the parish, and the world. Helping them to connect the dots in this way can pave a way that more naturally leads them to use their gifts in the service of others.

- **Being aware that mercy is something that each of us needs, and it is also something that we need to offer to others.** God gives it freely and gives us the help we need to give it to others too. But we have to work at it and welcome His help.
  - **How parents and parish ministers can help:**
    - Making regular Reconciliation a priority will help them see that they need mercy and grace. We all do, because we are human, not because we are "failures."
    - Read aloud the story of the Prodigal Son, and pray together. Use art (Rembrandt is beautiful) to help. Remind them that the father in this story is God the Father, who doesn't want or expect us to be perfect. He just wants us all to come home.

- **Seeing that all of their progress and achievements have come, not only from their own hard work (though that is certainly true too), but also from the help and sacrifice of many others.** The goodness and generosity of others have helped them achieve and get to where they are now.
  - **How parents and parish ministers can help:**
    - Help them practice and cultivate a habit of gratitude. Trace all of the good things and opportunities in their life back to someone else.

- Help them combat pride by seeing that every talent and gift they have has been given to them by the Lord.
- Hang this Scripture passage from James 1:17 somewhere visible: "Every good and perfect gift is from above, coming down from the Father of the heavenly lights, who does not change like shifting shadows."

- **Learning that "being" is just as fruitful as "doing" and helping them continue to assess whether they're making or holding the space to be with the Lord,** which sometimes requires slowing down and/or saying "no" to some things.
  - **How parents and parish ministers can help:**
    - Create space at home and in parish offerings specifically for silence, not just an absence of noise, but a silence that welcomes the Lord to speak, move, and be present.

- **Being patient with others who are less able or less driven.**

They can respond to and share the Lord with others by...

- **Recognizing that, to whom much is given, much is expected.**

- **Recognizing that their growth and accomplishments are meant to be a source of truth to others**—a "win" for the Church and for the world, not just for themselves.

- **Working hard on behalf of others and allowing their abilities and giftedness to serve others.**

- **Using their drive and their steadfast, committed spirit to advocate for, teach, stand up for, coach, and protect others,** especially those who are less able and less fortunate.

- **Using their natural leadership abilities to make things happen in their family, parish, or community.**

Do you want to explore a different cluster? Just head back to p. 34 to find the master list of all cluster options and their pages.

Or are you ready to move on to the next step in the process? Go to p. 36 to start "Becoming Food for the World."

James 1:17

"Every good and perfect gift is from above, coming down from the Father of the heavenly lights, who does not change like shifting shadows."

Scriptures and saints that might be particularly relatable and relevant

1 Kings 19:11-13	Bl. Benedict Daswa
Proverbs 3:5-8	Bl. Chiarra Bodano
Isaiah 41:10	Servant of God Dorothy Day
Ezekiel 36:26-27	Servant of God Leonie MArtin
Matthew 5:44	St. Jean de Brebeuf
Mark 10:42-45	St. John Bosco
John 13:13-17	St. Nicholas
Romans 5:8, 8:28	St. Pio of Pietrelcina
1 Corinthians 9:24, 10:13	St. Theresa of the Andes
Galatians 6:9	St. Augustine
Ephesians 6:10-11	St. Francis de Sales
Philippians 3:12-14, 4:13	St. Ignatius of Loyola
Colossians 3:2	St. Jerome
1 Thessalonians 5: 16-18	St. Joan of Arc
2 Timothy 4:7-8	St. Oscar Romero
James 1:2-4, 1:12, 1:17	Sts. Paul and Peter
1 Peter 3:15	St. Scholastica
1 John 4:16	St. Thomas More
	Venerable Teresita Quervedo

"I press on toward the goal to win the prize for which God has called me heavenward in Christ Jesus."

Venerable Teresita Quevedo

As a child, Teresita was known, not for her sanctity, but for her temper and strong will. After making her First Communion, a change started to take root in her, and at 10 years old she wrote,

"I have decided to become a saint."

With all of the strong will and determination in her nature, she pursued that goal passionately. She knew that becoming a saint meant allowing God to grow her more truly into herself. She was fun, energetic, and full of life - captain of the basketball team, voted "best dressed," and even an avid bullfighting fan. She wholly cooperated with God so that she could become who He had created her to be: wholly herself...indeed, her holy self.[5]

F. Attributes: Analytical, experimental, logical, pragmatic.

These individuals are likely craving *Truth*, particularly as it manifests in the tangible world—things they can measure, observe, study, and understand. They believe in and are attracted to things that make sense, and they want to understand God and His Church as much as they can. They want proof of His existence, His Goodness, and His power.

They will be searching for authorities on truth and reality. They benefit from recognizing that there is room for theory and speculation while studying creation, but that there is also objective truth that applies to all of us. This truth comes from the Lord Himself, the One who is Truth.

The Holy Spirit can guide them to think of science as exploring the world that God created, as opposed to something entirely other than God. He will likely be pouring out gifts of wisdom, understanding, and knowledge, if only they will welcome and cooperate with Him.

"Anyone who seeks truth seeks God, whether or not he realizes it."

They might benefit from praying like this...

- **Seeing how the Mass is rooted in salvation history and Scripture itself.** It will help Mass become more "true" and valid for these individuals.

- **Solid study of Scripture:** seeing what Scripture asserts to be true and what it doesn't (don't let the "7 days of creation" be a stumbling block to faith, when the Church doesn't even hold that the universe was actually created in seven 24-hour days!), and how the Old Testament prepared God's people for all that Jesus would do, say, and establish. Connecting the dots will be important for these individuals. There are patterns in how God operates, which help us to understand Him better and welcome Him more fully to operate in our lives too.

- **Becoming "friends" with other faithful scientists and intellectuals and seeing how their own pursuit of truth led them to and was supported by a relationship with the Lord and Church.**

- **Seeing history as a pattern; everyone who has come before us was part of God's plan to fulfill His promises.** Every brilliant discovery builds on others that came before it. And we are part of that plan too; we have been created to play some real part in His work of salvation and discovery.

- **Thanking God in an intentional way each time they learn something new or fascinating.** This helps connect the dots in their own minds and hearts that God delights in our study of creation, and He can guide our study and help us to understand and discover even more if we let Him.

- **Practicing gratitude forces us to see patterns of goodness outside of ourselves** goodness that connects us to others (past and present), that is intentional, part of a plan bigger than ourselves, and yet draws us up into it.

Scan QR code for more prayer guidance

ablazefamily.org/obt-prayer-guide/

- **Difficulty recognizing Jesus as the authority on truth.** He claimed to be "the way, the truth, and the life." C.S. Lewis said that we have to decide whether Jesus is a liar, a lunatic, or actually the Lord, the One He claims to be. There are no other options.
  - **How parents and parish ministers can help:**
    - Discuss with them that Jesus claims to have all authority in Matthew 28:18-20. He proves authority over the natural elements when He calms the sea and walks on water. He proves authority over sickness when He heals people. He proves authority over death when he raises the little girl and Lazarus, and He Himself is raised. The disciples died as martyrs to defend all of these stories as true.

- **Trouble seeing prayer, the liturgy, and the Sacraments as more than ritual. Help them appreciate that these are integrated expressions of confidence and hope in God.**
  - **How parents and parish ministers can help:**
    - Help them see how our behaviors are rooted in our beliefs. For example, we wash our hands before we eat, even if they aren't visibly dirty, because we believe in germs. When we believe something to be true, we act in a way that respects that truth. And since our belief in God is not just our own personal belief, but we are part of a community of faith, a communion of saints, we have "actions" that we do together.

- **These individuals might struggle with prayer experiences that seem to revolve around or lead to strong emotional responses.**
  - **How parents and parish ministers can help:**
    - Help them recognize that emotional responses to the Lord are valid, even if they're not typically this person's own experience, and that the Lord comes to us in many other valid ways too.

- **To them, personal testimonies and "subjective" experiences of God might not carry as much weight as more concrete, "objective"**

proof of God. Subjective experiences prove to us that God is Who He says He is; He doesn't ever claim to be a distant reality that we need to acknowledge. He claims to be our Father, deeply invested in our lives. That truth manifests in our lives in real, subjective ways.

- **How parents and parish ministers can help:**
  - Helping them articulate their own personal, subjective experience of God (even privately) will help these individuals see that the God Who is true is invested in their real lives.

- **Difficulty appreciating misunderstandings of science or creation from the past, understandings that colored the way the Church operated in history.** Recognize that having access to the fullness of truth and properly ***understanding*** the fullness of truth are not one and the same. As is always the case with the Lord, understanding unfolds over time, and we need the Holy Spirit's help.
  - **How parents and parish ministers can help:**
    - Liken it to a suitcase full of everything it will ever hold that is being unpacked over time. People in the "unpacking" stage early on only see some of what's in there. People who come later have the benefit of knowing what others have already unpacked, but also seeing more as they continue to unpack.

- **Being impatient with those who are more drawn to goodness rather than truth and those who are in need of goodness and mercy, but don't necessarily feel their need for truth.**
  - **How parents and parish ministers can help:**
    - Help these individuals see that the truth we believe necessarily leads us to action: God is good (this is true and measurable), He has been so good to us (also true and measurable, you can make a list), and in His Goodness, He invites us to participate in His Goodness to others.
    - Just as God doesn't require us to be deserving before He is good, in inviting us to participate in His Goodness, He asks us to extend the same grace to others.
    - Help them pray for patience, understanding, and mercy. We don't have to "fake it 'til we make it." He can and wants to help!

They can respond to and share the Lord with others by...

- **Sharing their own passion for truth in a way that helps connect the dots for others.**

- **Helping others know that wrestling with truth is a good thing, as long as we keep pursuing truth.**

- **Using their pursuit of truth to develop understandings, teachings, products, and opportunities for the good of others.**

- **Gently helping others pursue goodness that is rooted in truth, particularly truth revolving around the inherent dignity of the human person.**

Do you want to explore a different cluster? Just head back to p. 34 to find the master list of all cluster options and their pages.

Or are you ready to move on to the next step in the process? Go to p. 36 to start "Becoming Food for the World."

John 8:32

"Then you will know the truth, and the truth will set you free."

Scriptures and saints that might be particularly relatable and relevant

Deuteronomy 6:4	Blaise Pascal
1 Kings 3:5-14	Bl. Benedetta Bianchi Porra
Psalm 111:10, 139:13-14	Bl. Carlos Acutis
Proverbs 1:7, 2:6-7, 15:33, 18:15	Bl. Francesco Faa di Bruno
Luke 2:19, 10:27	Bl. Nicolas Steno
John 8:32, 14:6	Servant of God Takashi Nagai
Romans 11:33	Servant of God Jerome Lejeune
1 Corinthians 1:25	St. Albert the Great

Saints (continued)

Colossians 2:2-3
James 1:5, 3:17
1 Peter 5:5

St. Anatolius of Laodicea
St. Augustine
Sts. Cosmas and Damien
St. Gianna Mola
St. Giuseppe Muscati
St. Isadore of Seville
St. Luke
St. Matthew
St. Thomas Aquinas

Servant of God, Takashi Nagai

Dr. Takashi Nagai lived in Japan in the early 1900s. He was a scientist, who specialized in the theories of atomic structure and nuclear fission. He was also an atheist, at first.

After experiencing his own restlessness and meeting Catholics and Christians who clearly found meaning in life that all of his studies couldn't, he seemed willing to admit that they had something he wanted. He was inspired by the writings of Christian scientist Blaise Pascal, and after boarding with a Catholic family in Nagaski, his fate was sealed. That family's daughter would become his future wife, and she prayed fervently that he would find the truth he was seeking in Christ and His Church. In 1934, after much wrestling with faith, he was baptized and they were married.

Takashi's wife was killed in 1945 by the atomic bomb that struck Nagasaki; ironically, it was the same technology that Takashi had spent his life studying. He took comfort in his faith; He spent the rest of his life determined to serve those who had been impacted by the horrific radiation from the bombing and bearing witness to the truth that God is calling us to live in peace. [6]

G. Attributes: Compassionate, cooperative, helpful, peacemaker.

These individuals are likely to be craving **Goodness**, especially as it manifests in justice, mercy, and kindness extended toward others and themselves.

They are likely to encounter the Lord through His justice and mercy, in a way that feels personal and real, allowing them to see and recognize how He has been so good to them. Not just good in general, which He is, but good to them personally.

Their lives can be radically transformed when they ask the Holy Spirit to help them see God's Goodness in their lives, as it comes directly from Him and through others. And when they ask Him for right judgment and courage: the ability to know what is truly right and the power to do it.

"Help one person at a time and always start with the person nearest you."

They might benefit from praying like this...

- **Practicing gratitude deeply by paying attention and "taking stock" of their blessings in a way that allows them to see with greater clarity how good the Lord has been to them, in big and small ways.** This helps them see, in tangible ways, how the Lord sees them, knows them, and loves them.

- **Expressing gratitude to the Lord directly as the next step in recognizing their blessings.** Making a habit of saying "thank you" to Him in their hearts can be part of the way they can "pray constantly," as St. Paul tells us.

- **Reading and pondering stories of the Good Shepherd (the One who gives His life for His sheep and seeks out the lost one) and the Prodigal Son (the Father who runs to meet us when we return home).** Meditating on these stories and using their imagination to enter into them can be very helpful.

- **Praying the sorrowful mysteries of the rosary and Stations of the Cross**, as they see that God will do and has done everything to save us; He thinks that each of us was worth every bit of the sacrifice. His mercy abounds—the meeting of our misery and need with His own heart!

- **Pondering and experiencing His mercy in a tangible way as we observe Baptism and experience Reconciliation,** where His indescribable Goodness and mercy are poured out on us and become the source of mercy and goodness that we can extend to others.

- **Recognizing that we can be generous and kind because He was generous and kind to us first.** "We love because He first loved us" (Romans 5:8).

Scan QR code for more prayer guidance

ablazefamily.org/obt-prayer-guide/

- **Sometimes, individuals who crave and show goodness might be tempted to think that truth is opposed to goodness (because sometimes truth hurts and seems unkind).** For them, truth must be intentionally cultivated, because they might not be drawn to it naturally. Goodness without truth might become something that is not authentically good at all.

2 Corinthians 12:9

"My grace is sufficient for you, for my power is made perfect in weakness." Therefore I will boast all the more gladly about my weaknesses, so that Christ's power may rest on me.

- ○ **How parents and parish ministers can help:**
  - ■ Help them see the connection between truth and goodness in God first; the truth is that He is merciful, and that manifests in His offering us mercy. The truth is that we are sinners in need of salvation, and God is just, so our sin can't just go ignored. It must be forgiven and remedied, and that's why Jesus came to save us. truth and goodness always flow into and out of each other; they are two sides of the same coin.
  - ■ God created us, so He knows what is really good for us and what will make us happy. The Commandments He gave us can seem hard, but they will always lead to our greatest happiness and to eternal life with Him in Heaven, because following them is part of what enables us to become more truly who He made us to be. That applies to every person, not just to Catholics. God made each of us.
  - ■ Help these individuals see that the goodness they already love so much is rooted in what they believe to be true: people matter, people deserve love, and people have dignity.
  - ■ Expose them to authentic Catholic Social Teaching, so they can see that the Church takes a very real stance on how we can be good and why that goodness needs to be rooted in objective

truth. Paragraphs 1928-1948 of the Catechism of the Catholic Church is a good place to start.

- **Feeling overwhelmed by a desire to show goodness so much that they feel like changing the world is all up to them.**
  - **How parents and parish ministers can help:**
    - Help them see how small acts of great love, given in a personal way by being present to one person at a time, is how the world changes. Help them find examples of this in the world around them. Look at the life of St. Teresa of Calcutta and how she treated each person individually and with a smile. If she had seen the people as a project or program, she wouldn't have achieved so much good. But the love she showed for each person was magnetic, attracting others to her way of life, giving dignity to the people she met, and furthering God's kingdom on earth.
    - None of us can do all things, except God, and He isn't asking us to do everything by ourselves or to replace Him. He's inviting us to share in His mission. He is the Savior, so we can take that pressure off of ourselves.
    - Ask the Holy Spirit every day: "What part do you want me to play in your great work of saving the world today?"

- **Being tempted to think that they don't have a deep relationship with God because their faith might not be as "exciting" as other people's might seem.** As Theodore Roosevelt once said, "Comparison is the thief of joy."
  - **How parents and parish ministers can help:**
    - Remind them that the Lord has created them on purpose, with a purpose: to be loved by Him, to love Him back, and to help share that love with others, all in a way that is unique and personal. He never compares us to others. Lean into the truth that each of us is chosen, called, and loved.
    - Ask them about their prayer life and their relationship with the Lord. Affirm what is good even if it seems small or limited.

- Ask them about their prayer life and relationship with the Lord. Affirm what is good, even if it seems small or limited. Cultivate and feed what is there, so that it can grow.
- Hang signs, stick post-it notes, leave messages with encouragement from Scripture and saint quotes where these individuals can see them. They'll likely need this consistent encouragement and reminder that the Lord is with them, whether they feel it or not.

- **Becoming an activist for justice without being rooted in a deep life of prayer.** Because God is Goodness itself, we can never separate Him from the process of doing good.

- **Avoiding conflict.** Nobody likes conflict (at least, nobody should) but sometimes conflict is necessary in order to reach true peace, and live by true justice and mercy.
  - **How parents and parish ministers can help:**
    - Help them gain confidence in the fact that they are absolutely loved by God and that He is calling them to be His hands and feet. The goodness they strive to offer is not their own work; it is a participation in His work. There is freedom there because when others disagree with us, they're not disagreeing with us, but with Him. And He's big enough to deal with it.
    - Model for them how to have healthy and respectful disagreements and conversations. Have them at home so that they learn how to stand their ground without feeling like (or becoming) a bully.

They can respond to and share the Lord with others by...

- **Saying to the Lord, "Send me," throughout the day.** Asking God where it is that He is calling them to bring His Goodness and love to the those around them in big and small ways. This helps keep them rooted in love, because Christ first loved us. It keeps Jesus as the source of, the power behind, and the ultimate end of the love that we share.

- **Offering others what God offers to all of us: to be seen, known, and loved**. Smiling, learning people's names, acknowledging them, and looking others in the eye.

- **Being reminded, and reminding others, that "the small ways" are often much bigger than we realize.**

- **Accompanying those who suffer or struggle, to show them that they are not alone.** This is what Jesus does for us, He who is Emmanuel, God with us. Be empowered to answer suffering with love.

Do you want to explore a different cluster? Just head back to p. 34 to find the master list of all cluster options and their pages.

Or are you ready to move on to the next step in the process? Go to p. 36 to start "Becoming Food for the World."

1 Peter 4:10

"Each of you should use whatever gift you have received to serve others, as faithful stewards of God's grace in its various forms."

Scriptures and saints that might be particularly relatable and relevant

Psalm 86:15	Bl. Chiara Badano
Proverbs 4:23	Bl. Pier Giorgio Frassati
Isaiah 49:13	Servant of God, Dorothy Day
Zechariah 7:9	St. Aloysius Gonzaga
Matthew 7:12, 9:36-38, 19:26	St. Damien of Molokai
Luke 10:30-35	St. Elizabeth of Hungary
Galatians 5:22-23	St. Francis of Assisi
Ephesians 4:32	St. Gemma Galgani
Colossians 3:12-13	St. Jeanne Jugan
1 Peter 4:10	St. Joseph Cupertino

St. Katharine Drexel

St. Martin de Porres

St. Peter Claver

St. Teresa of Calcutta

St. Vincent de Paul

St. Martin de Porres

St. Martin de Porres was a simple man. He was treated poorly, because he was born out of wedlock and was the mixed-race son of a freed slave. But he had a heart that was well aware of God's Goodness to him, and as he welcomed and cooperated with God in His Goodness, he began to serve others. He volunteered with the Dominicans and did menial tasks that nobody else wanted to do. But in so doing, he shared God's love with everyone he met. He welcomed everyone, rich and poor, healthy and sick, and became a sign of God's love in a powerful way. [7]

Fr. Henri J. M. Nouwen

"For most of my life I have struggled to find God, to know God, to love God. I have tried hard to follow the guidelines of the spiritual life—pray always, work for others, read the Scriptures—and to avoid the many temptations to dissipate myself. I have failed many times but always tried again, even when I was close to despair. Now I wonder whether I have sufficiently realized that during all this time God has been trying to find me, to know me, and to love me. The question is not 'How am I to find God?' but 'How am I to let myself be found by him?' The question is not 'How am I to know God?' but 'How am I to let myself be known by God?' And, finally, the question is not 'How am I to love God?' but 'How am I to let myself be loved by God?' God is looking into the distance for me, trying to find me, and longing to bring me home."

H. Attributes: Affectionate, expressive, outgoing, talkative.

These individuals are likely craving **Goodness**, particularly as it manifests in the expression, demonstration, and articulation of love, relationships, emotions, and experiences. They likely feel "fed" by spending time with others.

They are most likely to encounter the Lord in ways that are expressive and dynamic, ways in which they can feel loved by Him.

The Holy Spirit can help these people know for certain that they are loved and treasured by God, and that He is calling them to be part of the way that He loves and treasures others too. Through His gifts of courage and right judgement, He can inform their emotions and intuitions so that they know the right thing to do, and have the power to do it.

> "Be who God meant you to be and you will set the world on fire."

They might benefit from praying like this...

- **Opportunities to pray with others in ways that are dynamic and expressive, like themselves:** praise and worship, liturgy with incense, candles, and lots of visible and sensible expressions.

- **Reading and praying through Scripture with a guide (either a person or a bible study guide/series) that helps them reflect and apply it to their own lives,** to experience for themselves that Scripture is truly living and effective.

- **Journaling as a way to express their prayer and discern how God is responding.**

- **Growing comfortable with aspirations (i.e. "thank you, Lord!", "You are good, Lord!", "Amen!") will give them the freedom to express their prayers to the Lord in real-time.**

- **Practicing mental prayer as an ongoing conversation with God,** who makes Himself present and available to us at all times and places.

- **Learning Ignatius' Rules for the Discernment of Spirits,** especially recognizing how our emotional lives interact with our spiritual lives. View our full "Playbook for the Spiritual Life" series at *setusablaze.tv/programs/playbook*.

Scan QR code for more prayer guidance

ablazefamily.org/obt-prayer-guide/

Potential prayer/spiritual blind spots or challenges...

- **They might encounter the Lord with great emotion, and that might become their "measuring stick" for encountering Him at all.** Emotions are neutral in and of themselves. While they are sometimes the way that the Lord makes Himself known to us, but they certainly are not the only way. As C.S. Lewis put it,

"The great thing to remember is that, though our feelings come and go, God's love for us does not."

- ○ **How parents and parish ministers can help:**
  - ▪ Make space in your family to talk about emotions and to process them together. Allow these individuals to "feel their feelings," while walking with them in discerning what to do.
  - ▪ Help these individuals be rooted in something more stable and constant than emotions—the truth that God loves us always, whether we feel it or not—while still valuing their place in prayer and spiritual life. Help them seek evidence of this truth in beauty.
  - ▪ Help them memorize Scripture passages that keep them rooted in this truth. Memorizing Scripture allows it to become part of the "script" in our own minds, influencing our thoughts and actions.
  - ▪ Give them access to Ignatius' Discernment of Spirits to help them recognize valid movements of the Spirit, even in times that are less emotionally enjoyable.

- **Difficulty appreciating and practicing silence, since they might not be naturally inclined toward it.**
  - ○ **How parents and parish ministers can help:**
    - ▪ Help these individuals see that silence actually gives God room to speak to us; He isn't silent at all! Share with them different insights and inspirations that you've had in silence so that they have evidence that it can and does bear fruit.
    - ▪ Start small with one or two minutes of silence. Help them learn how to "dump" their thoughts, cares, concerns, hopes, and dreams to the Lord, and then sit and listen. This will help them get potentially distracting thoughts out of the way first.

- **They might be tempted to put much expectation on human relationships to bring their deepest fulfillment.** This leads to disappointment, as no human can ever possibly love us perfectly. Only God can.

- How parents and parish ministers can help:
  - Tell them that God's love alone is perfect, but also help them experience God's love in a real way so that they have a relationship with Him. Seeing how Jesus is portrayed in *The Chosen* television series can help make Him more real and relatable to older kids and teens.
  - Help them cultivate a relationship with the Holy Spirit. Learning to recognize His prompting and presence will give them greater assurance of His constant care and abiding friendship.

- **Difficulty cultivating a personal prayer life, one that is sustainable with or without the presence of community (as has been needed during the COVID-19 quarantine).** Practice makes progress.
  - How parents and parish ministers can help:
    - Expressing their prayers and thoughts in a journal might be a helpful way for them to still be expressive, even if there is nobody else there besides the Lord to hear them.

They can respond to and share the Lord with others by...

- **Setting a tone/creating a culture of friendliness and making others feel welcome.** Others will likely look to them to set the tone in group settings, and being inclusive, inviting, and hospitable goes a long way to help someone know that they matter and they are loved.

- **Recognizing that God loves them (and all of us) even when they don't feel it and offering love to others.** They can help others to know that that's normal and healthy.

Do you want to explore a different cluster? Just head back to p. 34 to find the master list of all cluster options and their pages.

Or are you ready to move on to the next step in the process? Go to p. 36 to start "Becoming Food for the World."

"Do not forget to show hospitality to strangers, for by so doing some people have shown hospitality to angels without knowing it."

Scriptures and saints that might be particularly relatable and relevant

1 Kings 19:11-12	Bl. Carlo Acutis
Esther 4:14	Bl. Pier Georgio
Proverbs 16:24	Pope St. John Paul II
Matthew 9:35-36	St. Augustine
Mark 16:15	St. Catherine of Siena
Philippians 1:6, 4:4-9	St. Dominic
Titus 2:7-8,	St. Francesco Spinelli
Hebrews 4:16, 13:2	St. Francis of Assisi
	St Hildegard of Bingen
	St. John Bosco
	St. Josemaria Escriva
	St. Philip Neri

Bl. Pier Georgio

Pier was a hiker, mountain climber, student, jokester, and a lover of Jesus and His Church. He had a big laugh and an even bigger heart. In many ways, he was larger-than-life. He was exuberant and joyful, and he served others with gusto. He was generous with his attention and love, serving others by giving *himself*, not just time or money (though he was generous with those too). His ability to see, know, and love others wasn't just his own human ability, and he knew it. He said this:

"The faith given to me in baptism suggests to me surely: by yourself you will do nothing, but if you have God as the center of all your action, then you will reach the goal[B]

I. Attributes: Easy-going, happy, makes friends easily, optimistic.

These individuals are likely to be craving **_Goodness_**, particularly as it manifests in joy, fun, humor, and friendship. They tend to recognize good qualities in others (and hopefully, in themselves too). They enjoy laughter and bond with others through it.

They are often sunshiny, "silver lining" individuals, the ones who recognize good, even in less-than-desirable situations.

The Holy Spirit's gift of courage can help them to boldly share their joy with others.

"There is nothing on earth more to be prized than true friendship."

They might benefit from praying like this...

- **Spending time relating to Jesus as a faithful friend, the One who sticks with us through thick and thin.**

- **Learning how to have conversations with Him in their heart, ongoing throughout the day.**

- **Praying the joyful mysteries of the rosary and the Magnificat.** Praying with daily devotionals will help them see and experience that God is with them everyday.

- **Keeping a gratitude journal will help them see how God is consistently good,** even if He doesn't always do what we ask Him to do.

- **Reading and meditating on encouraging Scripture passages will be edifying.** It will help them see and know that God is with them and for them.

- **Studying Scripture and seeing how God consistently brings order out of chaos, good out of lack, and light in the darkness.** He is trustworthy and worthy of our praise.

- **Coming to a solid understanding of Theology of the Body (in age-appropriate ways) to see how God made them good, in His image and likeness.** Our friendships, relationships, and bodies are ways that we can give glory to Him.

- **Befriending saints, who were intimate, personal friends with God.**

Scan QR code for more prayer guidance

ablazefamily.org/obt-prayer-guide/

- **It's important for them to know that God delights in them, that they are chosen by Him.**
  - How parents and parish ministers can help:
    - Help these individuals memorize and pray with what He says to and about them, which is the same thing He said to and about Jesus at His Baptism: "And a voice from heaven said, 'This is my Son, whom I love; with him I am well pleased'" (Matthew 3:17).

- **Sometimes these individuals go above and beyond to please others.**
  - How parents and parish ministers can help:
    - Help them see that the One Person we need to strive to please is God, by being faithful to Him and loving others as He does.
    - Teach them Ignatius' practice of a Daily Examen before bed, to invite the Holy Spirit to walk back through each day with us, seeing when and how we responded to His promptings and when we didn't.

- **Rejection can feel especially heavy to these individuals.**
  - How parents and parish ministers can help:
    - Stand with them if and when they experience it, allow them to feel what they feel, and offer them the truth that God has not and will not reject them. He can work all things for good, even when a situation seems hopeless.
    - Help them cultivate healthy, Christ-centered friendships. No human friend will be perfect, but having Christ-centered friends will more likely mean friendships that are (mostly) free of unnecessary drama.

- **These individuals might have a difficult time with commandments, laws, or precepts that seem unkind or make people feel sad.**
  - How parents and parish ministers can help:
    - Remind them that what God asks and demands of us is always for our good. Trusting in Him means that we might not always understand it, but He is still trustworthy.

- **Encouraging others; visiting the sick, suffering, and homebound.**

- **Being a steady friend.**

- **Helping to diffuse tense situations.**

- **Accompanying those who suffer or struggle with doubt,** helping others see how the Lord is present and good, even in times of trial and hardship.

- **Serving with children, particularly those who might be shy or afraid to leave their parents.**

- **Sharing joy with others in a way that brings levity and silver linings to difficult situations.**

Do you want to explore a different cluster? Just head back to p. 34 to find the master list of all cluster options and their pages.

Or are you ready to move on to the next step in the process? Go to p. 36 to start "Becoming Food for the World."

1 Chronicles 16:32-34

"Let the sea resound, and all that is in it; let the fields be jubilant, and everything in them! Let the trees of the forest sing, let them sing for joy before the Lord, for he comes to judge the earth. Give thanks to the Lord, for he is good; his love endures forever."

Scriptures and saints that might be particularly relatable and relevant

Psalm 16:11, 20: 4-5, 95: 1-2	Bl. Chiara Badano
1 Chronicles 16: 32-34	Bl. Pier Giorgio Frassati

1 Samuel 18: 1-4	Pope St. John Paul II
Matthew 5:9	St. Elizabeth of the Trinity
John 15:10-11	St. Faustina
2 Corinthians 9: 6-8	St. Francis of Assisi
Philippians 4: 4-8	St. John Bosco
	St. John the Apostle
	St. Josemaria Escriva
	St. Lawrence
	St. Philip Neri
	St. Thomas More

St. John Bosco

St. John Bosco John was a priest, and his first assignment was in Turin, Italy, where he found many teenage boys roaming the streets and getting into trouble. The solution at the time was to arrest them, but John had another idea; he wanted to befriend them. He juggled and did circus tricks to attract them and earn their trust, and then welcomed them into real friendship with himself, so that he could invite them into real friendship with Jesus. His mother helped him, and they began finding work and lodging for these boys whom Jesus loved so much. He said,

"It is not enough to love the children, it is necessary that they are aware that they are loved." (9)

Appendix B

Feeding Through Developmental Stages

I. Children Up to 7 Years Old

Toddlers and young ones tend to have a strong sense of wonder, often craving *Beauty*. They want to be awed and amazed by God in a way that they can explore through their five senses and imagination.

Our role in helping them encounter the Lord during this stage is as their main "feeder." Similar to how infants and toddlers need us to help put food into their mouths, it's our job during this age and stage to be intentional about both exposing them to beautiful things and pointing out what we think is so wonderful about them. This season involves a sort of "spoon feeding" and "follow the leader" approach, as our kids need us to do much of the work and prompting.

We also need to make sure "feeding time" (any potential encounter with the Lord) is gentle and pleasant. The context in which we help them encounter teaches them as much as the encounter itself.

Note: Children learn quickly that church, prayer, and God are boring if that is their experience.

- **Take them outside to experience the beauty of creation, and tell them explicitly that God is the One who made it all.**
    - Give them time to watch ants and wonder how they are so strong.
    - Put out some birdseed, watch all the different kinds of birds that come and go, and marvel alongside them at the birds' beauty.
    - For early risers, watch the sunrise and tell them that God reminds us each day that He is with us.
    - Make a habit of watching the sunset together as a family, and appreciate how each one is different.

- **Expose them to amazing art (not just "kid art").**
    - Play beautiful music for them, not just "kid music."
    - Hang sacred images at their eye level. For babies, this might be up high for them to see as you carry them around. For toddlers and children ages 3-6 years old, hang the sacred art a few feet off the ground.
    - Take them to see big, beautiful churches (virtually or in person).

- **Cultivate silence (even little spurts) in your home so that their imaginations have time to be active.**
    - Ask them questions that help them to wonder.
    - Tell them simple Bible stories and show them art that depicts those stories, and then sit and ponder with them.
    - Dim the lights and light candles when you pray, so that they know something special is happening now.
    - Read good literature to them.

- **Develop family traditions around birthdays, baptism days, holidays, and Holy Days, etc.** Let them participate in the decorating and celebrating.

- **Saturate their senses with all things beautiful, and explicitly tell them that everything beautiful reminds us of God.** He made our senses of smell, sight, sound, touch, and taste so that we could experience beauty with our whole bodies.

- **Pray aloud with them at set times like before meals and bedtime, but also as you encounter beauty through your senses.** It can be as simple as, "What a beautiful sunset; thank you, Lord!" or "I love the smell of snow; thank you, Lord!" Model for them how to welcome and recognize God throughout the day in planned and spontaneous ways.

- **Take them with you to Sunday Mass each week, and invite them to notice the beauty all around—the music, art, and kind people gathered to pray with you.** Point to the Eucharist when the priest elevates it and whisper, "There's Jesus!" Light a candle and pray for something that matters to them. Teach them to use their senses to enter into the Mass, even if they're too young to really know what's happening. Invite them to see that God comes to meet us at Mass.

Read on to learn about feeding through other stages.

Ready to start exploring the attribute cluster(s) and flavor preferences? Go to p. 34 for the full list.

Do you want to go back to the process? Return to p. 36.

Or do you want to start "Encountering the Lord in the Everyday"? Go to appendix C on p. 114 for the full list.

II. Children Ages 8-13 Years Old

Children in this age group tend to add a strong desire to know what is real and true to their still active sense of wonder. Their brains are starting to develop in a way that will impact what they believe for the rest of their lives, and they are often craving **Truth,** in addition to their own personal inclinations.

In this age and stage, our kids' brains are beginning the process of shedding old connections and forming new neural pathways, a process that will continue throughout adolescence.[1] While younger kids might be more likely to trust what they've been told, children in this stage are more inclined to question what they've been told is true. It's good news that scientists have discovered that it's never too late for our brains to change (neuroplasticity), but these children are naturally in a season ripe with brain change, and we should leverage that! They are forming a sense of reality out of which they are likely to operate for the rest of their lives.

As they outgrow the fairytales and magic of their earlier childhood, we need to ensure that they don't "outgrow" their faith. We need to help them see that God really is good, that He really did make them good, that He really does have a plan and really does have authority. And we need to invite them to come alongside us to see proof of it all—to see what we see.

Our role is to invite them to pick up a fork and eat what and how we're eating, standing next to us as we pursue and consume truth together. We introduce them to more robust spiritual food here, and show them how to chew and taste for themselves. Shoulder-to-shoulder experiences replace the follow-the-leader style in this stage.

- **Tell them the truth about who they are—children of God, created on purpose, with a purpose.** Affirm that they matter with what you say, and show them by being attentive and present.

- **Tell them true stories to help reveal who God is and how He wants to be at work in our own lives.** Read saint and Scripture stories that are true (we have suggestions in our sections about encountering God through literature and media on p. 127 and p. 162), and ask them how they see God working in a consistent way, here and now.

- **Pray with them about everything—the big things, small things, good things, and difficult things too.** Model for them, through prayer, that we have a God who actually cares about us, hears us, and is powerful enough to handle all of our concerns.

- **Start to connect, in an explicit way, what Jesus said to what the Church teaches to what you live out.** Help them see that because Jesus is trustworthy and He instituted the Church, we can trust the Church in her teaching of Faith and Morals. As our children start to understand why the Church believes and does what she does, it's okay to seek out answers together.

- **Pray as a family, and encourage individual prayer too.** Model that for them by carving out time for yourself to pray, and let them know that you are praying for them during that time.

- **Go to the Sacrament of Reconciliation as a family on a regular basis.** Show them that they can trust Jesus, who loves us. His mercy is bigger than any sin we have committed.

- **Encourage questions, even hard ones.** They're going to ask them anyway. It's better for you to make it clear from the start that they can always come to you with questions, instead of hiding them and seeking answers elsewhere.

- **Be consistent. Let them see that the same truth that you proclaim is the truth you are trying to live, and be ready to admit and apologize when you've fallen short.** You are showing them that all of us need God's grace and that all of us are works in progress who can ask forgiveness and start fresh.

- **As they hit this age, allow other trusted people to tell the stories that they need to hear, and come alongside them to listen as equals.** This way they have the opportunity to take just as much ownership of the truth as you do, and you can share your insights and inspirations together. Ask for that insight, seek it out, and by doing so, show them that they matter and that you care about their ideas.

- **Seek opportunities to have fun with them and to challenge each other, even if it's not overtly spiritual.** Bonding through fun and challenge builds trust and earns you the right to be heard in matters that are more serious.

- **Prepare for Mass on Sunday by praying with and talking about the readings in advance.** Listen to the *Enkindle: Family Scripture Reflections* podcast to help get the conversation started, and ask them what they hear the Lord saying to them in and through those readings.

Read on to learn about feeding through other stages.

Ready to start exploring the attribute cluster(s) and flavor preferences? Go to p. 34 for the full list.

Do you want to go back to the process? Return to p. 36.

Or do you want to start "Encountering the Lord in the Everyday"? Go to Appendix C on p. 114 for the full list.

III. Teenagers and young adults

Teenagers (14-18+ years old) tend to have a strong desire to become and be part of something meaningful. They are likely craving ***Goodness,*** in addition to their own personal inclination.

They want to be good at something, to belong with people who affirm their goodness. But even more than that, they are growing in their desire to be part of some good that is bigger than themselves. They are looking for a cause to make their own, and they need help to see how God is inviting them to participate in ***His*** Goodness, in a particular and personal way.

These youth will need an ever-growing community of other faithful believers (peers and especially adults) to help them to experience, respond to, and participate in God's Goodness. They need us to help them find peers and adults who can affirm their goodness even when they make mistakes.

They're becoming independent spiritual eaters, and they likely want to pick their spiritual foods and experiences more and more. But they still need us. We should keep inviting them to join us in encountering the Lord in His fullness; a balanced diet. And we should offer them and help them to seek opportunities to encounter Him alongside other people (youth ministers and groups, mission trips, etc.) too.

- **Help them find goodness that they're passionate about by asking them questions and seeking (spoken or unspoken) patterns in their answers.** Chapter VI (p. 36) can help with this.

- **Model for them how to participate in God's Goodness in small *and* big acts of kindness, in opportunities inside *and* outside the home.**

- **Help them live goodness in such a way that they feel not only a sense of accomplishment, but also a sense of being more fully alive.** That is a sign of the Holy Spirit at work, a sign that this is something to which He is calling, at least for now. And recognizing that sense will help them to discern what He might be calling them to in the future.

- **Volunteer alongside them to help find causes that excite them and make use of their talents and personalities.** Explore all kinds of ways that people serve God through the Church: contemplative or intercessory prayer, serving those in need (like the poor, elderly, or marginalized), teaching, lobbying for positive change, visiting prisons or group homes, ordained priests, lay volunteers, etc.

- **Show them that God made them unique in all the world with a purpose by helping them recognize their particular gifts, talents, interests, and helping them matching these with something meaningful for the good of others.**

- **Show them that God is merciful and always ready to forgive by being merciful yourself and keeping them connected to the Sacrament of mercy.** Making frequent Reconciliation a family affair before you get to this phase will allow them to seek mercy without it feeling "obvious" that they might need it now more than ever. Apologize when you need to, to show them you aren't perfect either.

- **Help your children learn how to recognize true goodness—Gospel goodness, rooted in Church teaching—by helping them find a trusted source that *they* like and respect.** Expose them to multiple, trusted sources of Catholic Social Teaching to help them find the one that most resonates with them. The same truth can feel different coming from a different mouth.

- **Have a special prayer opportunity that is just for you and them. Sometimes doing something at an unusual time adds to the "special."** A late-night holy hour, a special midnight Mass for New Years Eve, an early morning Mass for their baptism anniversary, or some other special way to grow closer to Jesus alongside them, at an hour that makes it all the more special for them.

- **Don't forget: have fun and laugh with the teens in your life!** Good fun goes a long way.

- **Continue to build a *cloud of witnesses* around all of your children, especially when they are teens.** Help them see different ways that people can live out their response to Jesus' invitation by surrounding them with diverse, faithful witnesses—people who are willing to laugh, cry, pray, and play with your teens. They need people who aren't afraid to share the story of what God has done for them and to accompany them as they welcome the Lord more deeply into their own lives too.

- **Seek opportunities that allow your children to serve, but also grow in their understanding of Catholic Social Teaching:** Catholic Work Camp experiences, mission trips, service weeks, and even just your own family-organized serving experiences where you tie a simple Truth about why we do what we do to the act of doing it.

- **Continue providing them with dynamic opportunities to grow and encounter God through *Beauty, Truth, and Goodness*.** Model for them that faith is a life-long growing process by growing yourself.

- **Help them develop healthy friendships with other people who are pursuing Christ.** Holy friendships are a manifestation and source of Goodness, and they become more important than ever for teenagers.

- **Keep praying.** Keep praying as a family, as individuals, with people from church, etc. Help your children encounter and be nourished by the Lord over and over in prayer. All of our efforts are for nothing if they aren't rooted in Jesus. Model John 15:1-8 for them: He is truly the vine, and we are the branches. He desires to bear great fruit in and through us, but we must remain in Him.

- **Keep going to Mass as a family.** Prioritize it, even on vacation and during school breaks. Help your teens see that Mass is where Jesus comes to meet us. It is worth whatever sacrifice and planning are necessary to get there and encounter Him.

- **Eat dinner as a family together.** Even as schedules get busier, don't give up on family dinners! Make sure that home is more than just a place to sleep and regroup before going out again. Make it a safe haven where they know they are seen, known, and loved. A place where they can share hopes, dreams, fears, regrets, and know that they can experience God's Goodness through you, no matter what.

Pope St. John Paul II

"It is Jesus who stirs in you the desire to do something great with your lives, the will to follow an ideal, the refusal to allow yourselves to be ground down by mediocrity, the courage to commit yourselves humbly and patiently to improving yourselves and society, making the world more human and more fraternal."[2]

Ready to start exploring the attribute cluster(s) and flavor preferences? Go to p. 34 for the full list.

Do you want to go back to the process? Return to p. 36.

Or do you want to start "Encountering the Lord in the Everyday"? Go to Appendix C on p. 114 for the full list.

Appendix C

Encountering the Lord in the Everyday

I. Cultivating Lifelong Eaters

1 John 4:19

"We love because He first loved us."

Our hunger for the Lord is nothing compared to His hunger for us! He loves us long before we even think about loving Him, and He comes to meet us in countless ways. We can have, and help others to have, a deeper, more satisfying relationship with the Lord by recognizing Him in the lives we are already living.

Just as our bodies need food multiple times per day, every single day, so we are nourished when we open our eyes and hearts to welcome the Lord as He comes to encounter us every single day.

On the subsequent pages, you will find several different ways that you (or anyone) can encounter the Lord or walk through "gateways" to encounter:
- Through prayer and the Sacraments (p. 116-126).
- Through literature (p. 127-133).
- Through the five senses (p. 134-142).
- Through nature (p. 143-148).
- Through family activities and traditions (p. 149-155).
- Through service (p. 156-161).
- Through music, podcasts, and other media (including special Bibles and devotionals) (p. 162-165).
- Through sports and competition (p. 166-170).

Recognizing and responding to the Lord in a way that integrates with our lives will allow us to be more fully nourished by Him, and ultimately, to grow into the unique and unrepeatable individuals that He created us to be.

Acts 17:26-27

"From one man he made all the nations, that they should inhabit the whole earth...God did this so that they would seek him and perhaps reach out for him and find him, though he is not far from any one of us."

A. Through prayer and the Sacraments

Prayer is recognizing and responding to Emmanuel, God who is always with us. It is opening the door to Him Who already seeks us. It is recognizing that the One Who desires us to share our hearts with Him has already poured out His heart for us. Even to respond to Him, we need His help! And He is oh-so-willing to give it.

St. Teresa of Calcutta

"Love to pray. Prayer enlarges the heart until it is capable of containing God's gift of himself."

As Catholics, many of us have learned our prayers, and that's important!

But how many of us have actually *learned* how to pray?

Different saints have defined prayer differently, and it might be helpful to hear what a few of them have to say to have a better understanding of what it really is, and how we can really do it.

The Catechism of the Catholic Church shares this from St. Augustine, as he reflected on the story of Jesus meeting the Samaritan woman at the well:

> CCC 2560
>
> "'If you knew the gift of God!' The wonder of prayer is revealed beside the well where we come seeking water: there, Christ comes to meet every human being. It is he who first seeks us and asks us for a drink. Jesus thirsts; his asking arises from the depths of God's desire for us. Whether we realize it or not, prayer is the encounter of God's thirst with ours. God thirsts that we may thirst for him."[1]

Referenced in the Catechism of the Catholic Church, St. John Damascene said that prayer is "raising one's heart and mind to God." [2]

"Prayer," said St. John Vianney, "is the inner bath of love into which the soul plunges itself."

The Catechism sums all of these up by saying that prayer is "the habit of being in the presence" of God.[3]

We need to help our children realize that prayer is ***not*** somehow summoning a God who otherwise wouldn't be paying attention.

117

As we learn how to spend time with and open our hearts to the Lord through different forms of prayer, we will discover ways that are a good "fit" for our own particular craving. **Remember:** *the Lord is trying to get our attention in a particular way, a way that correlates with our craving.* When we encounter Him in this way, we are most likely to experience a sense of wonder, joy, peace, and satisfaction.

When it comes to helping our children grow in their relationship with the Lord, we want to expose them to and model for them more and more forms of prayer so they can have a robust and diverse "diet" and be satisfied by God's love and presence in many ways. We also want to help them learn how to pray with others, so we have a special little section on family prayer too.

Here are some tried and tested forms of prayer. If some of these are new to you, that's okay! We have step-by-step guides in a downloadable PDF (just scan the QR code below with your phone). Find someone who prays this way frequently, and ask them why they love it. Find a saint who loved it, and ask them to pray for you as you learn to pray in this way.

Scan the QR code

1. Open the camera on your phone.
2. Hold your phone over the QR code, and make sure the code is in frame.
3. Tap the prompt when it appears, and it will redirect you to the webpage with the prayer guide PDF.

View-Only Version

Print Version

You can also find the prayer guide at
ablazefamily.org/obt-prayer-guide.

Personal Prayer

Try using some of the modes of prayer suggested in your attribute cluster or your children's attribute clusters. If those don't seem to be especially fruitful, then try any of the others listed below. Give it some time; all good things require practice.

The point is to allow ourselves to enter into conversation with God, to be surrounded by His loving presence, and to recognize that He is with us. This might come in a sensible feeling or emotion or in an awareness that leads to joy and peace. But sometimes, our prayer doesn't come with any palpable, tangible experience, and that's okay too.

When we enter into prayer that feels dry, we need to stay rooted in the truth that we know for sure: God is with us and for us, even if and when we don't feel and hear Him.

Family/Group Prayer

Humans are hard-wired to need community, and God provides for this need in our families and parish communities.

We pray as a community because

1. We aren't alone in our desire for living life to the full and striving for eternal life, or in being invited to encounter and respond to Jesus throughout the journey toward it.

2. Jesus promised that whenever two or more are gathered in His name, He would be there in our midst. And Jesus always keeps His promises.

3. Christ instituted the Catholic Church so that we could have access to Him, just as we are united with one another as His adopted family.

So pray with the Church family. Participate in Mass. Gather some friends and prayer a rosary. Fast with the Church during Lent and on Fridays. Pray with your family, group, and friends. Here are many ways to do that.

FOR THOSE WHO CRAVE BEAUTY

- **Ask the Holy Spirit to help find beauty:**
  - How does this experience inspire and stir a sense of wonder in you?
  - What can you do to fully enter into this beauty?

FOR THOSE WHO CRAVE TRUTH

- **Ask the Holy Spirit to help find truth in this experience (and hopefully share it afterward):**
  - What in this experience reveals and reflects truth?
  - How is He inviting you to respond to this truth?

FOR THOSE WHO CRAVE GOODNESS

- **Ask the Holy Spirit to help find goodness:**
  - What in this experience reveals and reflects God's Goodness?
  - How is He inviting you to participate in this goodness too?

Venerable Fr. Patrick Peyton

"The family that prays together stays together. A world at prayer is a world at peace."

The Sacraments: Nourishment for all of us

Unlike other forms of prayer, the Sacraments aren't something we are meant to pick from as an option; they lay a foundation of guaranteed encounter meant for all of us. Jesus gave us all seven Sacraments so that we can access Him through His Church spiritually *and* physically. Sacraments are part of the Lord's great plan of saving the world, nourishing us with Himself and growing us into who He created us to be.

St. John Vianney

"There is nothing so great as the Eucharist. If God had something more precious, He would have given it to us."

Most of the Sacraments are received only once, but two are given to us to access repeatedly: Eucharist and Reconciliation. Just as we need to eat multiple times each day, every day of our lives, we also need to regularly feed on God's grace and presence as He comes to us in these Sacraments.

In Reconciliation, Christ removes our sin, which blocks grace and starves us spiritually, and replaces it with His own life.

Of all the Sacraments, the Eucharist is called the "source and summit" of the Christian life. It is Jesus Himself—Body, Blood, Soul, Divinity—given to us as food that is both physical *and* spiritual.

Eucharistic Adoration

Bl. Carlo Acutis

"If we get in front of the sun, we get sun tans...but if we get in front of Jesus in the Eucharist, we become saints."

It's exactly what it sounds like: adoring Jesus Christ, truly present (Body, Blood, Soul, and Divinity) in the Eucharist. Every time we pray, Jesus comes to us spiritually. But in Eucharistic Adoration and the seven Sacraments, He welcomes us spiritually *and* physically.

"The Eucharist is the bread that gives strength... It is at once the most eloquent proof of His love and the most powerful means of fostering His love in us. He gives Himself every day so that our hearts as burning coals may set afire the hearts of the faithful."

Praying with Scripture: Meditation, Lectio Divina, Visio Divina

Hebrews 4:12

"For the word of God is alive and active. Sharper than any double-edged sword, it penetrates even to dividing soul and spirit...it judges the thoughts and attitudes of the heart."

When we read Scripture, we aren't just reading a story that was written a long time ago. We are reading God's words to us, here and now. Like He did for St. Augustine, God speaks to us personally in and through His Word.

Meditation and Lectio Divina are ways of reading and praying with Scripture that uses your imagination to lead you into the story itself, invites the Holy Spirit to guide you through the process, and allows you to hear God speaking to you through the passage.

Similar to Lectio Divina, Visio Divina uses art to help lead us into prayer. Again, we invite the Holy Spirit to guide us and speak to us through the image, as we use our imaginations to place ourselves in it.

Silence

St. John the Cross

"God's first language is silence"

This practice will be easier for some people than others, but it is necessary for all who hope to build a relationship with the Lord. In silence, we can truly hear Him speak and recognize His promptings more clearly. Silence isn't really silent at all; it's silencing everything else so as to hear Him.

Novenas

Dating back to the time between the Ascension of Jesus and the descent of the Holy Spirit at Pentecost, we spend nine days in persistent prayer and have confidence that the Lord hears us and provides for all of our needs. There are all kinds of novenas, including a Pentecost novena, just like the Apostles prayed!

Rosary

The rosary is a way of praying that invites the Blessed Mother to pray with and for us, while we meditate on key moments in the life of Jesus. Again, we invite the Holy Spirit to guide and lead us, as we imagine ourselves in the events and moments and come to know Jesus more intimately.

Divine Mercy Chaplet

Given by Jesus to St. Faustina in Poland during her visions in the 1930s, this simple, repetitive prayer begs for God's mercy, which Jesus revealed He wants to pour out upon us generously! 5-7 minutes is all it takes, and it is powerful. You can find multiple internet resources to help guide you and your family through the Divine Mercy Chaplet today.

Liturgy of the Hours

It is the "official prayer of the Church." It has been prayed by priests, religious, and thousands of other people around the world for centuries. As the bells of a monastery or abbey used to do for people in medieval Europe, it marks "the hours of each day and sanctifies the day with prayer."[4]

Praise and Worship Music

St. Augustine

"Singing is praying twice."

There's something about praying words combined with music that allows us to pray from a greater depth of our heart and allows us to experience the Lord more powerfully too. Sometimes seen as part of a more charismatic spirituality, *anyone* can praise and worship the Lord using song.

Sacred Music

We have a rich tradition of beautiful, sacred music. Gregorian Chant, Hymns, and other sacred songs are a beautiful way to enter into prayer and join with others across the centuries as we reach out to the Lord, who is already reaching out to us. You can search online for different offerings and find them on any platform where music is available.

Liturgical Year and Daily Mass Readings

Daily Mass is a great way to pray, and it's often available at convenient times! But even if you can't physically make it to daily Mass, you can still pray with the Scripture readings. These readings are prayed in every single Catholic Church everywhere in the world; it's a great way to enter into what the Lord is doing alongside your fellow "hungry hearts."

Intercessory Prayer

In Scripture, we read about a paralyzed man who was carried to Jesus by his friends. The crowds were huge and they couldn't get close, so they climbed onto the roof of the house that Jesus was in, ripped it open, and lowered the man down through the ceiling so that he could be close to Jesus. We can do this for others; we can bring our friends, family, strangers, and all the cares of the world to Jesus through intercessory prayer!

Prayers of Gratitude

James 1:17

"Every good and perfect gift is from above, coming down from the Father of lights..."

Everything good is a gift from the Lord, either directly from His hands or passed through the hands of others. Develop an awareness of all the good that He has given you by practicing gratitude: a way to see through the lens of wonder, so that you can better recognize God at work. (We offer a special, family-friendly series on how to grow in gratitude in a way that is both practical and life-changing on *setusablaze.tv/programs/gratitude*.)

"...the great saint may be said to mix all his thoughts with thanks. All goods look better when they look like gifts."

Aspirations

This just means praying as you feel inspired throughout the day. It can be as simple as, "Thank you, Lord!" when you see something beautiful, or a "Help me, Lord," when you feel especially overwhelmed. This is a great way to "pray without ceasing," as St. Paul urges us in his first letter to the Thessalonians. It is also a helpful way to stay rooted in the truth that the Lord is with us always, not just in planned times that we have set aside specifically for prayer.

The Way of the Cross

Also known as The Stations of the Cross, they walk us through Jesus' Passion and Death. These are often prayed on Fridays during Lent, but they can be prayed at any time. They help us remember how much Jesus suffered because of His love for us, and as St. Paul says, to remember that we have been "purchased at a price" (1 Corinthians 6:20). Jesus paid everything to ransom us from sin and death, because He loves us. You can look up various versions of the Stations of the Cross for different audiences.

Litanies

Some examples of litanies include the Litany of the Saints, Litany of Trust, and Litany of Humility.

Journaling and Art Response

It's not just in our spoken words that we can speak to the Lord; we can write and draw the conversations we have with Him in our hearts too! This might be especially helpful for those who are imaginative and creative, but it can be helpful for others too. Many saints kept prayer journals, and we've benefited greatly from the insight they received from the Lord in prayer!

Devotional books

Devotional books are great tools to help us journey closer to Jesus, either with a daily reflection or a process of growing in understanding over time.

Attend a Latin Mass or Mass in another language

Mass is the highest prayer of the Church, and it speaks powerfully to truth-lovers, beauty-lovers, and goodness-lovers! Sometimes, we can see and participate in it with fresh eyes if we go to Mass at a different parish or in a different language.

Pilgrimage

A pilgrimage is a journey to a place that has spiritual significance with the goal of growing spiritually. It can help remind us that our entire earthly life is meant to be one great pilgrimage, as we let Jesus lead us all the way to Heaven.

It can be to a local shrine or monastery, the Holy Land, the location of a Marian Apparition or birthplace of a saint, your local Cathedral...so many places can be pilgrimage destinations! A pilgrimage allows our bodies to join our souls in doing what our soul should already be doing: journeying ever closer to the Lord. It allows our bodies to be immersed in **Beauty, Truth, and Goodness**, as made manifest in the site you are visiting.

St. Therese of Lisieux

"The world is thy ship and not thy home."

Want to explore other ways to encounter the Lord? Read on or return to p. 115 for the full list of ways to encounter Him in the everyday.

Ready to return to the process? Go to p. 36.

Want to explore the attribute clusters? Go to p. 34 for the full list.

B. Through literature

Good literature can be a gateway to encountering the Lord, even if it's not about Him. Literature captures and expresses **_Beauty, Truth, and Goodness_** within the context of story, helping us to better understand and enter into the human condition, our common experience, and our universal hunger.

"That is part of the beauty of all literature. You discover that your longings are universal longings, that you're not lonely and isolated from anyone. You belong."

Good literature

1. Allows us to learn how to pause, appreciate, and recognize **Beauty, Truth, and Goodness.**

2. Shows us what can happen if we do or don't seek **Beauty, Truth, and Goodness.**

3. Engages our imagination in a way that helps to form our thought processes and our thoughts themselves.

Picture books

- *Last Stop on Market Street* by Matt De La Pena
- *The Rabbit Listened* by Cori Doerrfeld
- *So Tall Within* by Gary D. Schmidt
- *Hello Lighthouse* by Sophie Blackall
- *Drawn Together* by Minh Le
- *I Am Enough* by Grace Byers
- *Jabari Jumps* by Gaia Cornwall
- *Story Boat* by Kyo Maclear
- *Miss Rumphius* by Barbara Cooney
- *The Blackbird's Nest: St. Kevin of Ireland* by Jenny Schroedel
- *Mother Teresa and Mary* and other books by Demi
- *Saints: Lives and Illuminations* by Ruth Sanderson
- *St. George and the Dragon* by Margaret Hodges
- *Moonlight Miracle* by Tony Magliano
- *The Holy Twins* and many other books by Tomie de Poalo
- *The Weight of the Mass* and *Take it to the Queen* by Josephine Nobisso
- *Each Kindness* by Jacqueline Woodson
- *Before She Was Harriet* by Lesa Cline-Ransome

Books for children ages 6-9 years old

- *The Moffats* by Eleanor Estes
- *Phantom Tollbooth* by Norton Juster
- *The Saturdays (series)* by Elizabeth Enright
- *Half-Magic* by Edward Eager
- *Betsy-Tacy (series)* by Maud Hart Lovelace
- *The Little Princess* by Frances Hodgkins Burnett
- *The Wheel on the School* by Meindert DeJong
- *All-Of-a-Kind-Family (series)* by Sydney Taylor
- *Heidi* by Johanna Spyri
- *Misty of Chincoteague* by Marguerite Henry
- *An Echo of the Fae* by Jenelle Leanne Schmidt
- *Redwall (series)* by Brian Jacques
- *The Narnia series* by C.S. Lewis (middle/high school will like these too)
- *The Little House* books by Laura Ingalls Wilder
- *Our Place in the Universe* by Jason Chin
- *Bethlehem books*
- *Lives of the Saints* from Ignatius Press
- *Brilliant! 25 Catholic Scientists, Mathematicians, and Supersmart People* by David Michael Warren

Pope St. John Paul II

"It is He who reads in your heart your most genuine choices, the choices that others try to stifle."

Books for children ages 10-14 years old

- *The Wednesday Wars* by Gary D. Schmidt
- *The Arrow & the Crown* by Emma C. Fox
- *The Bronze Bow* and other books by Elizabeth George Speare
- *The Eagle of the Ninth* and other books by Rosemary Sutcliffe
- *Little Women* and other books by Louisa May Alcott
- *The War that Saved my Life* by Kimberly Brubaker Bradley
- *The Way of the Wilderking* by Jonathon Rogers

- *The Green Ember series* by S.D. Smith (older elementary & middle, even high school will like these)
- *Brown Girl Dreaming* by Jacqueline Woodson
- *Echo* by Pam Munoz Ryan
- *Anne of Green Gables series* by L.M. Montgomery
- *Out of My Mind* by Sharon Draper
- *Wrinkle in Time* and *Meet the Austins* series by Madeleine L'Engle
- *When You Reach Me* by Rebecca Stead
- *The Mother-Daughter Book Club* by Heather Vogel Frederick
- *Howl's Moving Castle* by Diana Wynne Jones
- *Bob* by Wendy Mass & Rebecca Stearn
- *Where the Mountain Meets the Moon* by Grace Lin
- *Gone-Away Lake* by Elizabeth Enright
- *Wishtree* by Katherine Applegate
- *The Invention of Hugo Cabret* by Brian Selznik
- *The Vanderbeekers of 141st St.* by Karina Yan Glaser
- *Beauty* by Robin McKinley
- *Number the Stars* by Lois Lowry
- *Ella Enchanted* by Gail Carson Levine
- *The Chronicles of Prydain* series by Lloyd Alexander
- *The Princess and the Goblin* series by George MacDonald
- *The Penderwicks* series by Jeanne Birdsall
- *Moon Over Manifest* by Claire Vanderpool
- *To the Heights* by Brian Kennelly (high school ages will enjoy this too)
- *The Hobbit* by J.R.R. Tolkien
- *The Will Wilder* books by Raymond Arroyo
- *The Ranger's Apprentice* series by John Flanagan
- *The Girl Who Drank the Moon* by Kelly Barnhill (high school ages will enjoy this too)

C.S. Lewis

"Literature adds to reality, it does not simply describe it. It enriches the necessary competencies that daily life requires and provides; and in this respect, it irrigates the deserts that our lives have already become."

Books for youths ages 14 and up

- *Scorpio Races* by Maggie Stiefvater
- *Crossover* and *Rebound* by Kwame Alexander
- *The Running Dream* and *The Secret Life of Lincoln Jones* by Wendelin Van Draanen
- *Small Acts of Amazing Courage* by Gloria Whalen
- *My Family and Other Animals* by Gerald Durrell
- *Girl of the Limberlost* by Gene Stratton Porter
- *Okay for Now* by Gary D. Schmidt
- *The Hiding Place* by Corrie Ten Boom
- *Code Name Verity* by Elizabeth E. Wein
- *One Day in the Life of Ivan Denisovich* by Aleksandr Solzhenitsyn
- *Spinning Silver* by Naomi Novik
- *Screwtape Letters, Till We Have Faces, Mere Christianity*, and *The Space Trilogy* by C.S. Lewis
- *Memories of Glass* by Melanie Dobson
- *I Am Margaret* series by Corinna Turner
- *The Blue Castle* by L.M. Montgomery
- *Sophie Scholl and the White Rose* by Annette Dumbach and Jud Newborn
- *A Time to Die series* by Nadine Brandes
- *100 Days of Sunlight* by Abbie Emmons (Christian YA romance)
- *To Kill a Mockingbird* by Harper Lee
- Jane Austen's works
- *The Song of Roland* (a medieval epic poem about friendship and just war)
- *The Lord of the Rings* by J. R. R. Tolkien
- *The Lord Peter Wimsey mystery series* by Dorothy L. Sayers
- *The Father Brown Stories* by G.K. Chesterton
- *The Cadfael mystery series* by Ellis Peters

Neil Gaiman, paraphrasing G.K. Chesterton

"Fairy tales are more than true: not because they tell us that dragons exist, but because they tell us that dragons can be beaten."

Fiction books for adults

- *The Divine Comedy* by Dante Alighieri
- *Pride and Prejudice* by Jane Austen (and other of her books)
- *A Man Called Ove* by Fredrik Backman
- *The Story of Arthur Truluv* by Elizabeth Berg
- *Shadows on the Rock* by Willa Cather
- *Death Comes for the Archbishop* by Willa Cather
- *The Brothers Karamazov* by Fyodor Dostoevsky
- *Middlemarch* by George Eliot
- *In This House of Brede* by Rumer Godden
- *The End of the Affair* by Graham Greene
- *The Power and the Glory* by Graham Greene
- *The Space Trilogy* by C.S. Lewis
- *Station Eleven* by Emily St. John Mandel
- *Spinning Silver* by Naomi Novik
- *The Complete Stories* by Flannery O'Connor
- *Keeper of the Bees* by Gene Stratton Porter
- *My Name is Asher Lev* by Chiam Potok
- *Dear Mr. Knightley: A Novel* by Katherine Reay
- *The Lord Peter mysteries* by Dorothy L. Sayers
- *The Guernsey Literary and Potato Peel Pie Society* by Mary Ann Shaffer & Annie Barrows
- *Miss Buncle's Book* by D.E. Stevenson (and other of her books)
- *The Lord of the Rings* by J.R.R. Tolkein
- *A Gentleman in Moscow* by Amor Towles
- *Kristin Lavransdatter* by Sigrid Undset
- *Brideshead Revisited and Helena* by Evelyn Waugh
- *Tending Roses* by Lisa Wingate (and other of her books)
- *The Spear* by Louis de Wohl (and other of his books)

J.R.R. Tolkien

"The chief purpose of life, for any of us, is to increase according to our capacity our knowledge of God by all means we have, and to be moved by it to praise and thanks."

Nonfiction books for adults

- *Confessions* by St. Augustine
- *The Boys in the Boat* by Daniel James Brown
- *The Everlasting Man and Orthodoxy* by G.K. Chesterton
- *The Seven Deadly Sins: a visitor's guide* by Lawrence S. Cunningham
- *Deep Conversion, Deep Prayer* by Thomas Dubay (and other of his books)
- *The Shadow of His Wings* by Gereon Goldmann
- *The Lamb's Supper* by Scott Hahn (and other of his books)
- *84 Charing Cross Road* by Helene Hanff
- *Unbroken* by Laura Hillenbrand
- *The Creed in Slow Motion* by Ronald Knox (and other of his books)
- *Summa of the Summa* by Peter Kreeft (and other of his books)
- *Screwtape Letters* by C.S. Lewis (and other of his books)
- *Searching for and Maintaining Peace* by Fr. Jacques Philippe (any of his books)
- *The Introduction to the Devout Life* by St. Francis de Sales
- *Theology for Beginners* by Frank Sheed (and other of his books)
- *Life of Christ* by Fulton Sheen
- *Story of a Soul* by St. Therese

Flannery O'Conner

"Don't let me ever think, Dear God, that I was anything but an instrument for your story—just like the typewriter was mine."

Want to explore other ways to encounter the Lord? Read on or return to p. 115 for the full list of ways to encounter Him in the everyday.

Ready to return to the process? Go to p. 36.

Want to explore the attribute clusters? Go to p. 34 for the full list.

Through the five senses

God made us, body and soul, on purpose. And He desires that we encounter Him in our bodies and in our souls. Our bodies are often the doorway through which He walks to get to our souls, and chances are He is already coming to you in ways that you can sense; you might just not have realized it was Him!

When He became man, Jesus showed us that He wants to be with us in ways that we can see, touch, hear, smell, and taste. He spent His days teaching and preaching, touching and healing, and loving in a way that could be seen, heard, and felt. And that wasn't just for the people of His time; He wants to come to *all* of us, in all times and places, in ways that we can experience in and through our senses.

The most obvious manifestation of this is through the Sacraments, given to us by Jesus so that we could all have physical and spiritual access to Him. But all of creation has a sacramental nature to it, full of objects and experiences that point to and reveal something about the One who made it all. And all of our lives can be full of experiences through our senses that can point back, and even connect us with, the One who created us with those senses.

Psalm 34:8

"Taste and see that the Lord is good; blessed is the one who takes refuge in him."

Food, music, vistas and views, textures and temperatures and smells—all of these have the power to draw us to the Lord, if we allow the Holy Spirit to help us see how He's feeding us through them.

In a special way, God can work through our physical bonds with the people we love to allow those people to both experience our love *and* His!

The way you love your children is their first proof of God's love for them, and the parent/child relationship often impacts and informs their relationship with Him.

John 1:14

"The Word was made flesh, and dwelt among us."

Jesus was born in Bethlehem 2,000 years ago, and He is still here. He is here in the Sacraments and in the sacramental-ish: the ways in which we can see, touch, hear, smell, taste, or imagine anything that is true, or good, or beautiful.

Beauty

- **Fill your space with visual beauty: sacred and secular art, group photos that capture happy memories, souvenirs from happy times, family heirlooms, etc.** Let the walls of your home tell the story of God's love for you! Research indicates that "souvenirs" have the most powerful way of helping us remember. These include any physical objects—a hospital bracelet from when a baby was born or when someone experienced healing, a rock from an especially fun day at the park—and other things that might not be typical "display" items.

- **Fill your space with beautiful sounds:** music (sacred and secular, instrumental, etc.), cheerful greetings when your children come in, laughter together as you share jokes and play games, etc.

- **Along that vein, sometimes silence is the most beautiful sound.** We all need it, and the world does everything it can to make silence feel awkward or like "emptiness." But silence can be so rich and full, because it allows us to hear the Lord speaking. Cultivate silence in a way that feels inviting, instead of in a way that is just void of sound. Light candles, turn off screens, light a fire, whatever it takes to make silence feel lovely instead of empty.

- **Allow periods of silence to be part of your family culture.** It doesn't have to be just at home; it can be times in the car, while out for a hike or a walk, entire days carved out for your family to enter into silence. But start small. And afterward, ask each other and share with each other what you "heard" or experienced in your hearts during your time of silence. You will likely need to model the benefits of silence for children, unless they are ones who already enjoy it.

- **Fill your home with beautiful touch: hugs for comfort and congratulations, playful taps and tickles, and cozy snuggles.** Offer positive, wholesome touch even when you're angry or disappointed; don't let it be something that you withhold or that is perceived as being reserved only for when you're happy. Holding their hand or putting your hand on their shoulder while gently admonishing can help them realize that your love is there no matter how they behave.

- **Talk to your kids about their favorite smells, and tell them yours.** Make an effort to bring those smells into your family's life regularly, so they know that you remember and care about what they said.

- **Smell is actually the sense that is *most* tied to memory; it can trigger memories more than any of our other senses.** Create memories of love and faith around smells. If you can, find a Mass that uses incense and make the whole day special, so that every time you smell incense you think of that day. Smell chrism oil on newly baptized and confirmed people, and intentionally tie that experience to positive experiences of family and faith.

- **Notice (and help your kids notice) how the air smells different when it's about to rain or snow.** Notice how the earth smells different in winter, spring, summer, and fall.

- **Go to a farm or zoo together, and take notice of the foul smell. See how sometimes life is stinky, but it's still beautiful.** Sometimes, the stink is a sign of life. Also remember, as you smell the stench, that Jesus was born in a stable, surrounded by stink and filth. He wasn't afraid of it then, and He's not afraid of it now; He's not afraid or deterred by our mess either!

- **Make authentic cuisines on feast days of saints who are important to you or your family.** Enjoy the different cultural experiences of those who've been called to holiness, just like us.

- **Make your children their favorite foods for their birthday, Baptism day, Confirmation day, and any other day worth celebrating!** Allow their taste buds to be confident of your love for them and to be grateful for the variety of delicious flavors that the Lord has created.

- **Hug your children long and often.** But for those who don't love physical touch, find ways to touch that make them feel comfortable and safe.

- **Proclaim your love for your children verbally and in notes and texts.** Let there be no doubt that you love them, even when (perhaps, especially when) they've messed up or done something wrong. Let them know that the love of the Father is real and is made manifest in your own love for them.

- **Cozy up to read books watch movies, and laugh at funny memes with your children.** Link your family's media consumption with physical closeness and a shared experience to open more doors for communication and bonding.

- **Ask your children often what they heard, saw, smelled, touched, and tasted that was proof of God's love to them, and share your insight too.**

- **Periodically visit your local cathedral, basilica, shrines, or other churches for Mass and explore them.** Take in the different decorations they have and the different music they offer. See how it's the same as the Mass at your home parish, but with different beauty. Discuss things you notice. There are no right or wrong answers.
  - Does one type of music help some of you to pray more deeply?
  - Does one type of environment feel more welcoming?

Pope St. John Paul II

"He is waiting for you when nothing else you find satisfies you; He is the beauty to which you are so attracted; it is He who provoked you with that thirst for fullness that will not let you settle for compromise..."

Truth

- **Truth needs to be taught explicitly.** But what inundates and feeds our senses repeatedly will also be perceived as truth, whether we like it or not. The subtle messages we learn are often more powerful than we realize.

  Be intentional about what television shows and movies you watch, what books and magazines you read, and what music you listen to. Find a style that you like and then fill it with truth-filled content.
  - When your children ask to watch something that could sow seeds of falsehood, let them know why you don't want them to watch it. Give them plenty of good content to consume (see our literature and media section on p. 127 and p. 162 for some good ideas).
  - Read books with your children. Listen to podcasts with them, and watch shows that are rooted in truth, not just documentaries and non-fiction (though truth-lovers will probably appreciate those).

- Watch, listen, or read any story that has underlying truth: the Goodness of God and His creation, the power of community, etc. Share with them what you liked about it, something you've never thought of before, or what it reminds you of, etc. You are teaching them to think critically by doing it with them and creating space for them to wrestle with, reflect on, and apply truth.

- **Talk to your children about how to know what is true and what is not.** The Church has authority because Jesus has authority, and He is actively at work in and through His Church. We can trust Church teaching, because we trust Jesus and the Holy Spirit, regardless of whether the leaders in the Church seem trustworthy (but let's pray that they are anyway). Discuss all of this with them.
  - What does the world offer as "authorities" or sources of truth?
  - What do they get right? Where do they fall short?

  Encourage dialogue and ask questions. Seek out faithful people who can mentor you, and be a mentor for others.

- **Seek others who believe in the truth as revealed by Jesus and His Church.** Surround yourself and your family with a *cloud of witnesses* who can share that same truth from their own authentic experience.

- **Make sure that your kids are being formally educated in the Catholic faith and have content that they enjoy.** Faith formation that feels out of touch or boring can do more harm than good. Consider being a volunteer in a program that they love and show them that it's important to you. This makes faith formation a shared experience and will give you plenty of good things to digest together.

- **As you learn about saints or Scripture, find pictures of the places where these individuals lived and events took place.** Find maps and photos of objects found and preserved. Read about their lives in context so that you can remember that these were real people who lived real lives that were far from perfect.

- **Help your children connect the dots with Sacraments. Start with physical signs that the Sacraments use.** Understand first what is easiest to understand: what do these physical objects do for us? Then, ask the Holy Spirit to help you see what God is doing now spiritually through these physical signs in and through the Sacraments.

- **Root yourself in this truth, even when it's difficult to believe: you are good because God made you that way, and He loves you.** Speak it to yourself, your children, and others. Write it and hang it somewhere visible. The world works very hard to convince us that we have to strive to earn our way to being good and loved, but it simply isn't true.

2 Corinthians 2:14

"But thanks be to God, who always leads us...and uses us to spread the aroma of the knowledge of him everywhere."

Goodness

- **Warm your children's clothes in the dryer on a cold day (if applicable).** Have cozy socks ready to go for them when they come in from being outside. Allow the temperature and texture of what surrounds them to communicate love.

- **Put throw blankets around your home, creating a way for family and guests to feel comfortable and welcome,** and reminding yourself that God surrounds you with His love too.

- **Intentionally carve out time to spend together one-on-one with each of your children: do their favorite activity, go on an adventure, take a walk, share a meal, sit and talk together, etc.** This creates space for them to experience that they are seen, known, and loved.

- **Anticipate your children's needs; notice when they've run out of toothpaste, outgrown their socks, need more pencils, etc.** It's such a little thing, and one that we certainly can't keep up with all the time, but to notice their need before they mention it shows them that we're paying attention. We can't perfectly know all that they need before they tell us; only God can do that! And you can make sure that they know that He always knows.

- **Find some inspiring and encouraging saint and Scripture quotes, and send them to your children via text, email, mail, etc.**

- **Find and hang inspiring quotes, art and pictures, and Scripture verses on walls, doors, etc., and swap them out every week (or at some other regular time interval).**

- **Involve your children (especially small children) in Christmas and birthday gift-giving.** Have them come up with ideas that they think others would like, and let them come shopping with you. Help them see that giving good gifts is something that God does for us, and He invites us to join Him in it!

- **Make a special food**—something that your family loves—with your kids to donate to a soup kitchen or nursing home as a sign of love to others.

- **As your children grow and develop interests and talents, affirm their progress, not their perfection.** And encourage them to think of ways to share their gifts with others.

- **Observe what it is that makes your children "tick."**
    - What gets them excited?
    - What are they passionate about?

Join in that with them if you can, and surround them with faithful people who share that same or a similar tick. Allow them to be mentored by other individuals who are passionate and faithful.

Matthew 20: 29-34

"As Jesus and his disciples were leaving Jericho, a large crowd followed him. Two blind men were sitting by the roadside, and when they heard that Jesus was going by, they shouted, 'Lord, Son of David, have mercy on us!'

The crowd rebuked them and told them to be quiet, but they shouted all the louder, 'Lord, Son of David, have mercy on us!'

Jesus stopped and called them. 'What do you want me to do for you?' he asked.

'Lord,' they answered, 'we want our sight.'

Jesus had compassion on them and touched their eyes. Immediately they received their sight and followed him."

Want to explore other ways to encounter the Lord? Read on or return to p. 115 for the full list of ways to encounter Him in the everyday.

Ready to return to the process? Go to p. 36.

Want to explore the attribute clusters? Go to p. 34 for the full list.

D. Through nature

Everything that God has made reveals something about Him. And unlike art, which tells us something about the artist but doesn't necessarily connect us to them personally, creation opens a door for us to encounter the Creator Himself, if we let it.

If we recognize (and help our children recognize) that the Lord is speaking something to us through creation, then we can see creation as a love letter from the Lord, one that we and the people we love can "read" every day.

Again, this will take the guidance of the Holy Spirit, who helps us to see things as they really are, in a way that our human eyes alone can't see without His help. Come, Holy Spirit...

"Say to God, 'How awesome are your deeds! So great is your power... All the earth bows down to you; they sing praise to you, they sing the praises of your name.'"

Here are some ways that you can recognize the Lord coming to meet you in and through nature:

Pope St. John Paul II

"The way Jesus shows you is not easy. Rather, it is like a path winding up a mountain. Do not lose heart! The steeper the road, the faster it rises toward ever wider horizons."

Beauty

- **Go on a nature scavenger hunt with your children to explore.** Pick up acorns, feathers, flowers, and other treasures. Bring them to the family prayer table and thank God for His gift of creation.

- **Go on walks and adventures with your family, and pray in thanksgiving afterward.** Be intentional about thanking the Lord for the opportunity and for creating this beauty with you in mind. It doesn't have to be long and drawn out. A simple, "Thank you, Lord, for loving us and giving us such beauty" works.

- **Watch snow falling (or a video of snow falling) together and think about the fact that every single snowflake is different.** Literally, no two are the same, ever. This is just one of a myriad of ways that the Lord manifests His infinite creativity. Isn't that amazing?

- **Overcome an obstacle, ideally alongside your children.** See that the same God who gave you the ability to overcome it, will help you overcome other obstacles too. "I can do all things through Christ who strengthens me" (Philippians 4:13).

- **Download the "sky guide" app to see where you are in relation to the rest of the solar system.** See the same stars and planets that have captivated humans for centuries. Realizing that, while we now know more about space than ever, we still know so little. Lots of room for wonder!

- **Watch a sunrise or sunset, ideally with your children. Notice how the colors change minute to minute.** Breathe deeply and know that God had you in mind when He created everything for this sunrise/sunset to be a reality.

- **Appreciate each season, and invite your family to do the same:**
  - Rain, bursting color, the sound of birds and the new baby animals everywhere, the smells of the different flowers as they bloom, and the smell of the earth as it warms up in the springtime.
  - The growth and sunshine, the sound of tree frogs and a thunderstorm, and the way it feels to step into shade after being in the hot sun during summertime.
  - The changing leaves, pumpkins, and crisp air, the simplicity and stillness of bare trees, the sound of geese flying south for winter.
  - The way snow transforms the earth, the sound of it crunching underfoot, the sound/sight of creatures, the way the whole earth seems to be sleeping and waiting for spring, and the way the darker months make you crave light.

Job 12:7-10

"But ask the animals, and they will teach you, or the birds in the sky, and they will tell you; or speak to the earth, and it will teach you, or let the fish in the sea inform you. Which of all these does not know that the hand of the Lord has done this? In his hand is the life of every creature and the breath of all mankind."

Truth

- **Pause and take note of the minute details in nature; point them out to your kids.** See how these details make a difference in the way creation operates. Start to develop eyes that notice the extraordinary complexity of creatures, with the help of the Holy Spirit, so that you can stand in awe of the Creator.

- Encourage your children to think of science as "exploring the world that God created," instead of something entirely other.

- **Look at the stars, the planets, and the moon together.** Know that the same God who made them, made you, and had you in mind when He made them.
  - "'To whom will you compare me? Or who is my equal?' says the Holy One. Lift up your eyes and look to the heavens: Who created all these? He who brings out the starry host one by one and calls forth each of them by name. Because of his great power and mighty strength, not one of them is missing" (Isaiah 40:25-26).

- **Go to a zoo, aquarium, park, or anywhere you can observe different animals together.** Allow yourself to be still and ponder the different ways that God made each creature for the life they live.

- **Find scientists who are Christian who can help explain creation from a Christo-centric perspective.** There are more of them than you might think! You can find good resources in the media section (p. 162).

- **Discover what the Catholic Church teaches and believes about creation, evolution, etc.** Many people don't understand what the Church believes, and thus wrongly assume that the Church doesn't believe in science. Find good resources in the media section (p. 162).

- **Notice the logical patterns in nature: the seasons, growth cycles, water cycles, etc.** These patterns serve a vital purpose: to help sustain life and a healthy environment and ecosystem. See and understand that order and patterns come from an ordered, logical source, and not out of chaos. See that the Lord Himself is logical and ordered.

- **Study human embryology.** See how much care and detail goes into every human life, how each one has a completely unique, unrepeatable set of DNA.
  - Why do you think God creates humans this way?
  - What can we learn about God from studying the way in which He made us?

- **Study elements together and see that the same basic elements make up all living things, yet we're all different.** How are humans different from any other creature? We believe that humans have intrinsic dignity and value, not because of what they do, but because it's how God made them, in His own image and likeness, on purpose with a purpose.

Goodness

- **Study an endangered species with your children.** Discuss why you think God made that species and what He might want you to do to help preserve it. Allow your children to help you make a plan.

- **Study climate change together.** What do we know for sure? What can we do about it? How can we maintain respect for the dignity of human life *and* the environment? Respect for human life and for the environment are *not* mutually exclusive, as some believe. We have an obligation to always respect human life and to care for the earth too.

- **Go on a hike together with the goal of cleaning up trash and debris, and invite your children and family to join you.** See how a little bit of teamwork can make a real difference!

- **Make a bird feeder in the wintertime with your kids, and hang it outside of a window so you can watch the birds together.** Read Read Matthew 6:25-26 together. Sometimes the Lord provides food for the animals through us. Sometimes He provides for others through us, and sometimes He provides for us through others. Regardless, He always provides.

- **Volunteer at a local animal shelter with your kids.** Help them see that every animal deserves to be loved and cared for and that God is inviting you into His plan by giving you the opportunity to love and care for the animals that He created.

- **Plant native plants or flowers that attract pollinators (and not just bees, but butterflies, birds, ladybugs, etc.) with your kids.** Watch the difference those plants make as you discuss how God made certain plants and animals to help us, and sometimes we need to help them.

- **Plant a vegetable garden or pot and have your kids help with the whole process, from choosing seeds to weeding, watering, and harvesting.** See that good soil grows good, healthy crops, and let them see how much work goes into growing and providing food. Let them delight in the different flavors and take pride in producing their own harvest. Tie it back to the parable of the sower and the seed, the vine and the branches, the call for laborers in the vineyard. Help them understand what Jesus is saying by experiencing and doing what Jesus did. Then, share some of your harvest with others by giving some to neighbors or friends or donating some to people in need.

St. Thomas Aquinas

"Sacred writings are bound in two volumes—that of creation and that of the Holy Scripture."

Want to explore other ways to encounter the Lord? Read on or return to p. 115 for the full list of ways to encounter Him in the everyday.

Ready to return to the process? Go to p. 36.

Want to explore the attribute clusters? Go to p. 34 for the full list.

E. Through family activities and traditions

Family traditions and activities tend to show up big around holidays, but it's also the small "traditions" that are built into our everyday lives that help our children feel safe, loved, and part of something big and wonderful.

When our family traditions are tied to God's "family traditions" in and through the life of the Church, we help our loved ones (especially our children) develop those bonds and that identity within the context of their faith as well.

"Preserve the warmth of the family, because the warmth of the whole world cannot make up for it."

Participating in family traditions and activities together...

1. Helps us bond with the people we love and create a deep sense of belonging.

2. Helps offer a sense of safety and stability with something consistent to anticipate and enjoy.

3. Helps create a rhythm to our seasons and days.

4. Helps create a foundational narrative in their minds (and ours!) that they matter, that we do things that matter together, and that they are part of something bigger than themselves.

The Jewish people of the Old Testament were people of ritual and tradition, and they made sure that they told the stories. They made sure that their children knew the promises that God had made and the miracles that He had worked for their people. They talked about these events in a way that was personal, "Let me tell you what the Lord has done for *me*," even if the event they were describing happened long before that person was even born.

For the Jewish people, "collective memory" was strong, and their kids knew they were part of the promises that God had made. They were part of the story that He was writing. The story of their ancestors was ***their own*** story in a very personal way.

We can develop a sort of collective memory too, in addition to our own personal memories. With a little intentionality and a habit of connecting the dots, we can find our place, and help our children find theirs, not only in our own families and parish families, but in God's family as well. Each of us is not only part of our own story, but is invited to play a part in God's great story of salvation.

Be encouraged! Even if you've never had many traditions or any sort of commonly expressed or shared faith within your family, there is much hope. While starting new traditions, talking about faith can be hard if you're not used to it, but now is still a great time to start. Having a common experience alongside your kids is a great way to start new things and give everyone a chance to take ownership.

Pope St. John Paul II, *Familiaris Consortio*

"All members of the family have the grace and responsibility of building day by day the communion of persons, making the family a school of deeper humanity." [5]

Beauty

- **Make beautiful things together!** Food, art, music, laughter, a welcoming home, a warm bonfire—all of these things are beautiful. They allow our bodies to enter into rest, comfort, and joy, and they invite our souls to do the same.

- **Create a rhythm of beauty that you and your family can count on.** Make a certain meal for certain celebrations, play a certain song on birthdays (besides just "happy birthday"), do a certain activity to celebrate New Years or the first day of summer break, use a certain dish or plate for the birthday boy or girl. These small but stable acts of love help cultivate a sense of belonging and love, and they allow the people in our lives (and us) to find rhythm in their lives and to look forward to each season (literal seasons and developmental ones too).

- **Encounter beautiful things together; help your children cultivate an appreciation for many types of beauty through their five senses.** Go to museums and zoos, concerts and plays (virtually or in-person), restaurants and food trucks, etc. See what your local library or local parks and recreation department have to offer as far as craft fairs or story-telling events. Read books or watch movies together (see literature and media sections on p. 127 and p. 162).

- **Make a habit of going outside and doing something together at least once during each season.** Notice the things that you appreciate about each season. Notice that beauty is often mingled with the mess.

- ○ Ponder this: how is this true in your own life?

- **Light candles together in church before or after Mass.** Remember that God hears us, sees us, and goes with us. Ask your children who or what they would like to pray for, and allow them to light their own candle for their intentions. Remind them that, just as the candle keeps burning even after we leave the church building, our love for God and His love for us keep burning, even after we leave the church building.

- **Host a party or gathering, and invite friends to share their own family traditions and the stories behind them.** For example, host a Christmas cookie exchange and have each family talk about the cookie they brought and why it's their favorite. Or host a potluck, and ask each family to bring something that is authentic to their heritage.

- **See new places, virtually or in person.** Marvel at the beauty of the universe, the world, and the people in it.

- **Create a ritual on or around New Year's Day to look back and appreciate the beauty in the year past, and look forward in confident hope to the new year ahead.** Model how to find God in what has happened over the past year for your kids, so that they can be certain that He'll be with them as we all move forward too.

- **Create a bucket list together.** Hopefully, you'll get to at least some of those things! But perhaps, even more importantly, you'll create a culture of dreaming, goal-setting, and sharing in each other's hopes and dreams. Include the Lord in all of it, offering the list of hopes and dreams to Him, trusting that He is the Giver of *all good things*.

- **Prepare for Sunday Mass by reading and reflecting on the Scripture passages together.** Share your insights with each others. Use our Enkindle podcast (available on *enkindlepodcast.com* or anywhere podcasts are available) to help you get started.

"The first blessing which God gave was for the well-being of the family."

Truth

- **Discover the background for your traditions.**
  - Which ancestors were involved in creating this tradition, and why is it important to keep it going?

- **Celebrate the liturgical year in small ways at home, and live the same cycle the Church is living, so that you can see that your faith is not just something you visit or do on Sundays.** It's something that is part of who you are and they are. Being consistent helps connect the dots in a way that communicates truth.

- **Read about the history and origins of common traditions and celebrations like St. Nicholas Day, St. Lucia Day, Thanksgiving Day, Three Kings Day, etc.** Find the meaning in the symbols of the foods and practices that are associated with certain feasts, and tie those back to real people and events that actually happened.

- **Find and notice opportunities to hear from other faithful people who are older: grandparents, aunts and uncles, neighbors, and fellow parishioners.** Invite people to dinner and ask them to share stories of their own faith and of collective memory, so that you can be encouraged by others who find themselves in God's story too.

- **Together with your family, create prayer traditions that help you live out faith in God at all times.** Pray with, for, and over one another when you are thankful, sad, worried, afraid, or suffering. Pray "without ceasing" and model giving thanks at all times, just like St. Paul, who wrote that from his miserable prison cell. See consistent faith in the Lord and confidence in His providence, power, and love. Even if you aren't feeling that way, pray in a way that allows the Holy Spirit to have room to build that confidence in you.

- **Even if truth isn't your own gateway to the Lord, make an effort to immerse yourself in the teachings of the Church, so that your children see that goodness and beauty need truth in order to be fully and authentically good and beautiful.** Help them see that *Beauty, Truth, and Goodness* are the three legs of a sturdy stool that they can stand and rely on.

- **Create a space in your home to display memories and signs of God's faithfulness.** These can be part of the collective memory (family heirlooms, etc.), or part of your own experience (mementos from meaningful experiences, etc). Physical objects play a special role in keeping the reality of what God has done in the past in our minds so that we can remember the truth of what He's done and have confidence in Him moving forward.

- **Use a Jesse Tree to help your family prepare for Christmas during Advent.** The Jesse Tree tells the story of how God promised the Savior to Adam and Eve and spent the next several thousand years getting the world ready to receive that savior, Jesus Christ.

Joshua 24:15

"As for me and my house, we will serve the Lord."

Goodness

- **Create a gratitude ritual with your children.** At every meal, once a week in the living room, or in the car on the way to Mass on Sundays, have each person share something for which they are grateful. Train their eyes to find proof of the Lord's Goodness, even in hard situations. Create space for sharing stories of His Goodness, giving thanks for it.

- **When you hear a siren or see first responders, pause and pray for them and whomever they are helping.** Entrust all of them to God's love and mercy, and ask the Blessed Mother to intercede for them as you pray a Hail Mary together.

- **Serve together as a family.** Remember that our own goodness flows out of and cooperates with His.

- **Speak openly and often about how God made every person on purpose and with a purpose.** Everyone has dignity, not because of what they do, but simply because He made them.

- **Say hello to people.** Remind your kids that God always sees us, and part of sharing His love with others means seeing and acknowledging them, even if they don't acknowledge us.

- **Serve one another.** Help them seek and find ways to show love for each other. For example, serving breakfast in bed, making cards for someone who has had a bad day, taking on someone else's chore as a way to show love, etc.

- **Engage your children in ways that you can conserve electricity and water and live life in a way that cares for the earth.** Remind them that God made the earth and has asked us to take care of it.

- **Include them in birthday planning for loved ones.** Help them learn how to show love and grow in their joy as they see the work and care that goes into celebrations.

St. Teresa of Calcutta

"It is easy to love the people far away. It is not always easy to love those close to us. It is easier to give a cup of rice to relieve hunger than to relieve the loneliness and pain of someone unloved in our own home. Bring love into your home for this is where our love for each other must start."

Want to explore other ways to encounter the Lord? Read on or return to p. 115 for the full list of ways to encounter Him in the everyday.

Ready to return to the process? Go to p. 36.

Want to explore the attribute clusters? Go to p. 34 for the full list.

F. Through service

Serving others is foundational to the teachings of Jesus. It's foundational to following Him and being the person that each of us was created to be. Whether Goodness is our favorite flavor or not, we are all recipients of God's Goodness and are called to share that with others.

> "The King will reply, 'Truly I tell you, whatever you did for one of the least of these brothers and sisters of mine, you did for me.'"

Our goodness is a participation in and extension of His Goodness. It's a way that we can help others to experience the love of God in a tangible way, to help them know that He sees them, knows them, and loves them. God made each of us in His own image and likeness. We have dignity, not because of anything we've earned or accomplished for ourselves, but because He created us with dignity. And this dignity is at the heart of Christian service. When we serve others, we remind ourselves and them that God made them, loves them, and died to save them.

Remember this

1. Any "goodness" apart from what God has done and is doing, isn't truly good, no matter how good the motive or intention is. Our efforts to offer mercy, justice, kindness, and compassion have to always be rooted in and measured next to the truth of Who God is, the laws He has given us for our own good, and the dignity of every human life.

2. There are oh-so-many ways to share God's Goodness with others!

Sometimes, the opportunity to share His Goodness with others comes as a surprise, like when someone needs help unexpectedly. It might feel like an inconvenience or interruption, but it's actually an invitation from the Lord to share His love and Goodness with others. There are also plenty of planned opportunities to serve: volunteering in a ministry at church, working at a soup kitchen, committing to a specific service project or event, etc.

We need to commit to *both* specific and scheduled opportunities to recognize invitations for goodness that the Lord sprinkles in our lives every day. And as always, the best way to help the people in our lives is to serve alongside them and intentionally point out when we recognize an invitation to share God's Goodness.

We can get better at recognizing when God has sent someone to serve us by practicing gratitude: intentionally pausing and asking the Holy Spirit to help us see God's presence and love more clearly, even as it comes to us in and through the people around us. It is life-changing to recognize and remember that He sees, knows, and loves us in and through others, and does the same for others through us too!

Matthew 20:28

"... the Son of Man did not come to be served, but to serve, and to give his life as a ransom for many."

Beauty

- **Volunteer to help with music ministry or share your musical talent with nursing home residents.**

- **Make cards or handmade gifts with your children for an elderly neighbor, nursing home residents, or homeless shelter.**

- **Coordinate a bake sale with your children, and donate funds to the St. Vincent de Paul Society or your local food bank to share beautiful treats with those around you.**

- **Create beautiful Catholic rosaries, jewelry, icons, etc. to sell at a church craft show together.** Donate the funds to a hospital/shelter.

- **Make blankets for Project Linus or coordinate friends and family to make blankets together to be donated to kids in the hospital.**

- **Volunteer to lead craft projects at a children's hospital, shelter, or after-school program.**

- **Include your children and have them participate in the menu planning and cooking for the week and for special gatherings.**

- **Play with younger children;** help them engage their imagination.

- **Organize a concert or talent show at a local soup kitchen, nursing home, or hospital respite home (like Ronald McDonald House).**

- **Organize a talent show at your church to help build community or raise funds for a need.**

St. Therese of Lisieux

"Miss no single opportunity of making some small sacrifice, here by a smiling look, there by a kindly word; always doing the smallest right and doing it all for love."

Truth

- **Volunteer to help teach at Vacation Bible School, faith formation, or bible study.** Showing your passion and knowledge for the truth helps invite your kids and others to recognize and believe truth as well.

- **Advocate for God's Truth by joining or starting a pro-life club or attending the March for Life in Washington D.C. or in your state with your children.** God created each human life, on purpose, with a purpose, and in His own image and likeness. He doesn't make mistakes. Life is worth defending and protecting.

- **Volunteer at a home for mothers in crisis.** Advocating for and serving the unborn and their mothers is a great way to accompany those mothers and babies and affirm that they are both worth protecting. Your diocesan pro-life office should have a list of local homes and ministries that serve mothers in crisis.

- **Volunteer to be a lector at Mass or to lead a prayer service in your faith formation program, and help others by proclaiming the truth of God's Word.** Individuals gifted at public speaking help others in the Church to really listen and hear what God is saying to them.

- **Learn how to have respectful dialogue or disagreements with others.** This may not feel like service, but it is; we can serve, respect, and be good to one another even (and especially) when we disagree.

- **Make a point each day to tell your children a good truth about themselves.** Highlight a way in which God's gifts to them have made your life better that day.

- **Make a point to write or call your grandparents or an elderly neighbor regularly.** Tell them how important they are to you.

St. Therese of Lisieux

"Everything, even sweeping, scraping vegetables, weeding a garden and waiting on the sick could be prayer, if it were offered to God."

Goodness

- **Make blessing bags or bag lunches for the homeless in your area together.**

- **Pray for others as a family,** asking God to comfort them and send people to be His hands and feet.

- **Take CPR or First Aid training,** so that you can be prepared to help others in need of assistance.

- **Volunteer to lead games at the pediatric unit of a local hospital or at kids programming in your own parish.**

- **Run in a charity 5K or participate in the Special Olympics Polar Plunge.** It's a great way to offer a small, physical sacrifice to help others.

- **Lead/participate with your children in an effort to clean up a polluted area nearby.**

"Serve one another in love."

- **Include your kids in helping a neighbor, new parent, or someone who is sick or hurt with chores, yard work, or childcare.** Look out for someone who could use some help, even if it's with a small task.

- **Have your children participate in your tithing by helping you choose the organizations to whom you give, and let them see you do it.** It's important for them to see us being generous.

- **Volunteer to assist with cleaning the grounds of your parish or church together.** Help your children see that this makes people feel welcome and helps them to know that God wants them here.

- **For pre-teens and teens, join with them in stepping into another person's shoes (in a safe, controlled way).** Do a food fast, sleep outside on the ground, give up electronic screens for a weekend, etc. Allow them to experience a tiny taste of what many people experience so that they can appreciate the struggle. Then, brainstorm and put into action ways to do something for people who experience poverty, homelessness, etc.

Remember: not all of us are called to lead a large service project. Keeping in mind the words of the saints can help us keep love as the focus of our service no matter how big or small:

St. Teresa of Calcutta

"Not all of us can do great things. But we can do small things with great love."

Want to explore other ways to encounter the Lord? Read on or return to p. 115 for the full list of ways to encounter Him in the everyday.

Ready to return to the process? Go to p. 36.

Want to explore more attribute clusters? Go to p. 34 for the full list.

G. Through music, podcasts, and other media

There are some great Catholic websites, podcasts, and media out there, and they can help you and your children serve to encounter the Lord!

We don't have to have all the answers or be great at generating all of the conversations on our own. In fact, as we've said elsewhere, there is real value in sharing the experience of learning and growing alongside the people in your life, shoulder-to-shoulder, as opposed to being the "leader." The shared experience helps each of us individually and all of us collectively to be rooted more deeply in the Lord's *Beauty, Truth, and Goodness*. It allows for greater personal ownership of faith and deeper bonding between us, as our human relationships are strengthened by a shared relationship with the Lord.

St. Augustine

> "Let us sing a new song, not with our lips but with our lives."

Here are a few resources that we have vetted, though there are certainly more out there. Don't be afraid to search for them.

For all ages

- **Covenant Eyes:** This is a great, online filtering and accountability program that can help keep children safe online. You can use it on multiple devices and create different filters for each person. Since the average age children are exposed to pornography is between 8-11 years old, dependable filtering software is really important. *www.covenanteyes.com*

- **FORMED:** An on-demand subscription service of movies, programs, audio, and books. Great Catholic content for all ages. *www.formed.org*

For children ages 5 years old and under

- **Catholic Icing:** This is a great website with ideas for crafts, saints, and liturgical celebrations to do with young children. *www.catholicicing.com*

For children ages 6-10 years old

- **Catholic Sprouts Podcast:** This is a great podcast to share with children especially. The little nuggets of faith will inspire all of you to learn more about the Catholic faith. *www.catholicsprouts.com*

- **Saint Stories for Kids:** Chantal Baros, creator of Shining Light dolls, records a podcast just for kids to explore a new saint each week. *shininglightdolls.com*

- **Enkindle:** This podcast contains short and practical Scripture reflections on the Sunday Mass readings to draw families deeper into the Word of God. The messages are easy to digest, practical, and made for families and people of all ages to enjoy together. *www.enkindlepodcast.com*

"Worship the Lord with gladness;
come before him with joyful songs."

For youth ages 11 years old and up

- **The Chosen TV series** is about the ministry and miracles of Christ, and it highlights the call of the Apostles. *Available for free via The Chosen app or YouTube.*

- **The American Scientific Affiliation is a group of Christian scientists.** They have an online quarterly magazine, blog posts, guest articles, etc. *www.asa3.org*

- **Watch or listen to Fr. Spitzer's Universe on EWTN or research content,** which answers questions about science, the Catholic faith, and reason. *www.magiscenter.com*

- **Bishop Barron** helps the viewer see that these things are actually connected. *www.reasonfaithscience.com*

- **Saints for Slackers Podcast:** These little daily inspirations give a 2-3 minute saint story each day. *www.spotify.com*

- **Fr. Mike Schmitz podcast:** Fr. Mike tackles questions about the Catholic faith in short, bite-sized pieces. He's engaging and fun! *https://media.ascensionpress.com/category/ascension-podcasts /frmikepodcast*

- **Ascension's "Bible in a Year" podcast with Fr. Mike Schmitz.** *www.ascensionpress.com*

- **Chastity Project** is an excellent resource for answering questions about purity from a Catholic perspective. The resources and podcasts here are engaging and really help us see the dignity of human love as planned by God. *www.chastity.com*

- **Leah Darrow's *Do Something Beautiful* podcast** highlights people who are doing things to help others encounter the Lord in their daily lives. It challenges listeners to carry Christ out into the world.

- **iBreviary app** is for praying the Liturgy of the Hours or the Mass readings of the day.

- **Hallow App** has all sorts of Catholic prayers and guided Lectio Divina on it, and it's great for the whole family. *www.hallow.com*

Ephesians 5:18-19

"...be filled with the Spirit, Speaking to one another with psalms, hymns, and songs from the Spirit. Sing and make music from your heart to the Lord..."

Want to explore other ways to encounter the Lord? Read on or return to p. 115 for the full list of ways to encounter Him in the everyday.

Ready to return to the process? Go to p. 36.

Want to explore the attribute clusters? Go to p. 34 for the full list.

H. Through sports and competition

St. Paul consistently uses sports metaphors to help the early Christians understand what it means to live the faith. Sports encourage excellence, hard work and discipline, teamwork, and humility. They provide an environment for individuals to work for goals beyond themselves and to be coached and guided by mentors who see with greater perspective.

Not only can we enjoy and excel at sports, but we can also truly use them as a way to pursue and encounter the Lord. As always, if we want to be able to encounter the Lord through sports, we need to ask the Holy Spirit for help.

We need to be intentional about pointing out how the Lord is in each situation, even sports, and modeling for our kids how He might be inviting them to see their hard work, team work, discipline, disappointment, and victory as a metaphor for the spiritual work that God is inviting them to be part of.

"Sports contribute to the love of life and teach sacrifice, respect, and responsibility, leading to the full development of every human person."

Beauty

- **Each and every time we participate in something good that is bigger than ourselves, we participate in beauty.** Recognize the beauty in being part of a team and being part of a community that is working together toward a common goal. This appreciation helps us better appreciate our Christ-centered communities, and it helps us to see that, as Christ-centered communities, we should be working together toward a common goal. This will help us have a deeper appreciation for Christ-centered friendships, family, and fellowship in general.

- **Winning is so satisfying, not because we have defeated someone else, but because we've achieved something that we haven't before.** We've seen the difference that hard work and teamwork make. Apply that same discipline in your prayer life. Recognize that God is ready to help us grow and become the people He made us to be; we can't do it without Him! But He also won't do it without us; we have to show up.

Philippians 2:3

"Do nothing out of selfish ambition or vain conceit. Rather, in humility, value others above yourselves."

Truth

- **Every game has rules and regulations.** Seeing the importance of rules can help us see that the universal truths that apply to all of us not only make sense, but also help us to be safe, be happy, and grow. The 10 Commandments, precepts of the Church, and social justice rooted in an authentic understanding of human dignity apply to each of us. They are revealed to us by God, and they are for our own good, even when they're hard to accept.

- *Each* member of a team plays a *part*; no single person carries the team. This is a great way to help our children see that God has a plan for each of us. All of our plans work together to help accomplish His bigger plans, and He wants to be at work in and through all of us.

- **Hard work leads to progress, not necessarily perfection.** It's important for each of us to know that progress is the goal in sports and in life. Nobody expects perfection from us—not our teammates, not our coaches, and certainly not the Lord.

- **Winning teaches us a lesson, and losing teaches us a lesson.** "All things work for good, for those who love the Lord" (Romans 8:28). Feeling like we are "losing" doesn't mean that the Lord has abandoned us or led us astray; it means you can learn something and grow.

- **Perseverance means we keep going, even when it's hard, when it's no longer fun, when we aren't seeing the "success" that we had hoped we would see by now.** It's necessary in sports, and it's certainly necessary in our lives. Our relationships with the Lord won't always be easy or feel good, just like all of our relationships will have times that are easy and times that aren't. But we persevere; we keep going. We know that hard times are temporary, and we don't give up.

Pope St. John Paul II

"It is Jesus who stirs in you the desire to do something great with your lives, the will to follow an ideal, the refusal to allow yourselves to be ground down by mediocrity, the courage to commit yourselves humbly and patiently to improving yourselves and society, making the world more human and more fraternal."

Goodness

- **Teams that encourage one another are likely to enjoy their time together more, whether they win or lose.** There's more to sports than victory on the scoreboard; sports should help us grow into better versions of ourselves. Look for opportunities to offer encouragement to teammates, and even opponents.

- **Gratitude means recognizing that we have been given good things by someone or something outside of ourselves.** No athlete is self-made; coaches, parents, teammates, and even referees (fair or unfair) help us to grow, learn, and become better. Learn to be grateful for the others who have poured into you.

Hebrews 12:1

"Therefore, since we are surrounded by such a great cloud of witnesses, let us throw off everything that hinders and the sin that so easily entangles. And let us run with perseverance the race marked out for us..."

For older children and teens

- **Pray before every sports practice or game, and offer it up for someone in need of prayer.** This can add meaning and purpose to your sport, and it's a great way to make it a gift to others.

- **Play sports/games with a spirit of joy and good sportsmanship.** This attitude towards competition is infectious and encourages others.

- **Cheer for your teammates, even if you have to sit out for a game.** Being there for your team, even when you can't play, strengthens the team as a whole and invites others to have an opportunity to compete.

- **When playing sports/games with younger kids, be a coach to them.** Help them learn the game and encourage them when they lose; it shows them that you care and motivates them to keep trying.

1 Corinthians 9:24-27

"Do you not know that in a race the runners all compete, but only one receives the prize? Run in such a way that you may win it. Athletes exercise self-control in all things; they do it to receive a perishable garland, but we an imperishable one. So I do not run aimlessly, nor do I box as though beating the air; but I punish my body and enslave it, so that after proclaiming to others I myself should not be disqualified."

Ready to return to the process? Go to p. 36.

Want to go back and explore the attribute clusters? Go to p. 34 for the full list.

"Late have I loved you, O Beauty ever ancient, ever new, late have I loved you! You were within me, but I was outside, and it was there that I searched for you. You called, you shouted, and you broke through my deafness. You flashed, you shone, and you dispelled my blindness. You breathed your fragrance on me; I drew in breath and now I pant for you. I have tasted you, now I hunger and thirst for more. You touched me, and I burned for your peace."

St. Augustine

References

For All Scripture References

New International Version. Bible Gateway, https://www.biblegateway.com/versions/New-
   International-Version-NIV-Bible/. Accessed 1 May. 2021.

Part 2: Offering the One Best Thing

*(1) Familiaris Consortio of Pope John Paul II to the Episcopate to the Clergy and to the Faithful of
   the Whole Catholic Church on the Role of the Christian Family in the Modern World,* (#11).
   Promulgated by Pope John Paul II. [Vatican City]: 1981.

(2) Lewis, C S. *Mere Christianity.* New York: Macmillan, 1960. Print.

(3) Catholic Church. *Catechism of the Catholic Church.* (1266, 1282), 2nd ed., Our Sunday
   Visitor, 2000.

(4) Berkman, Elliott T. "Why Is Behavior Change So Hard?" Psychology Today,
   Sussex Publishers, 20 Mar. 2018, www.psychologytoday.com/us/blog/the-motivated-
   brain/201803/why-is-behavior-change-so-hard.

(5) Familiaris Consortio, (38).

(6) Bengtson, Vern L, et al. *Families and Faith: How Religion Is Passed Down Across
   Generations.* Oxford University Press, 2017.

(7) Smith, Christian, and Melinda Lundquist Denton. *Soul Searching: the
   Religious and Spiritual Lives of American Teenagers.* Oxford University Press, 2011.

(8) Bengtson, Vern L, et al. *(see ref. 5)*

(9) Eckmann Powell, Kara. "The Sticky Faith Guide for Your Family: Over 100
   Practical and Tested Ideas to Build Lasting Faith in Kids." The Sticky Faith Guide for
   Your Family: over 100 Practical and Tested Ideas to Build Lasting Faith in Kids,
   Zondervan, 2014, pp. 97–98.

(10) Bengtson, Vern L, et al.

(11) Sample, Kenneth R. "The 3 Transcendentals: Truth, Goodness, &
   Beauty." Reasons to Believe, 2 Feb. 2021, reasons.org/explore/blogs/reflections/
   read/reflections/2021/02/02/the-3-transcendentals-truth-goodness-beauty.

(12) Saint Augustine. "The Third Book." *The Confessions of Saint Augustine,* The
   Harvard Classics, 1909, pp. 354–430.

(13) Catholic Church. Catechism of the Catholic Church, (41).

(14) Kreeft, Peter. "Lewis's Philosophy of Truth, Goodness, and Beauty." *IVP Academic,*
   Print on Demand Edition, 15 Jan. 2008.

(15) Michael, Chester P., and Marie C. Norrisey. Prayer and Temperament: Different
   Prayer Forms for Different Personality Types. *Open Door, Inc.,* 1984.

(16) Kreeft, Peter. (see ref. 2)

(17) "The Ages & Stages Of Child Development." *Child Development
   Institute,* 10 May 2020, childdevelopmentinfo.com/ages-stages/#gs.qnk3tt.

(18) "Temperament and Your Child's Personality." Child Development Institute, 23 July
   2019, childdevelopmentinfo.com/child-development/temperament_and_your_child/

(19) "Child Development: Ages and Stages." *CHOC Children's*, 21 July 2020, www.choc.org/primary-care/ages-stages/.

(20) *Pastoral Constitution On The Church In The Modern World — Gaudium et Spes.* Promulgated by Pope Paul VI. [Vatican City]: 1965.

Appendix A: Attribute Guide

(1) Quinones, Rachel, et al. "Moments with Multicutltural Saints: Josephine Bakhita // ACE at Notre Dame." Alliance for Catholic Education, 23 Aug. 2017, ace.nd.edu/news/moments-with-multicutltural-saints-josephine-bakhita.

(2) "Who Is Saint Benedict?" Saint Benedict Church, http://www.saintbenedict.org/saint benedict.

(3) "Saint of the Day - Blessed Fra Angelico." *Sacred Heart Parish*, 18 Feb. 2020, sacredheartseward.org/events/saint-of-the-day-blessed-fra-angelico.

(4) Nemo, John. "What a NASA Janitor Can Teach Us About Living a Bigger Life." The Business Journals, 23 Dec. 2014, www.bizjournals.com/bizjournals/how-to/growth-strategies/2014/12/what-a-nasa-janitor-can-teach-us.html.

(5) Hunter-Kilmer, Meg. "Fully Alive: The Little Terror' Who Wanted to Be a Saint." Aleteia, 20 July 2017, aleteia.org/2017/07/20/fully-alive-the-little-terror-who-wanted-to-be-a-saint/.

(6) Janaro, John. "Servant of God Takashi Nagai." Catholic Education Resource Center, www.catholiceducation.org/en/faith-and-character/faith-and-character/takashi-nagai.html.

(7) Catholic Online. "St. Martin De Porres - Saints & Angels." Catholic Online, www.catholic.org/saints/saint.php?saint_id=306.

(8) "Brief Biography of Bl. Pier Giorgio Frassati." FrassatiUSA, Inc., frassatiusa.org/frassati-biography.

(9) Catholic Online. "Popular Saints - Saints & Angels." Catholic Online, https://www.catholic.org/saints/saint.php?saint_id=6

Appendix B: Feeding Through Developmental Stages

(1) *Moskowitz, Clara. "Teen Brains Clear Out Childhood Thoughts." LiveScience, Purch, 23 Mar. 2009, https://www.livescience.com/3435-teen-brains-clear-childhood-thoughts.html.*

(2) *15th World Youth Day—Vigil of Prayer.* Address of Holy Father Pope John Paul II. [Tor Vergata]: 2000.

Appendix C: Encountering the Lord in the Everyday

(1) *Catechism of the Catholic Church*, (2560).

(2) *Catechism of the Catholic Church*, (2559).

(3) *Catechism of the Catholic Church*, (2565).

(4) "Liturgy of the Hours." *USCCB*, https://www.usccb.org/prayer-and-worship/liturgy of the-hours.

(5) *Familiaris Consortio*, (21).

Made in the USA
Coppell, TX
17 September 2023